THE GRAD'S GUIDE TO

HEALTHY LIVING

Mind, Body, Soul, Spirit

NavPress is the publishing ministry of The Navigators, an international Christian organization and leader in personal spiritual development. NavPress is committed to helping people grow spiritually and enjoy lives of meaning and hope through personal and group resources that are biblically rooted, culturally relevant, and highly practical.

For a free catalog go to www.NavPress.com
or call 1.800.366.7788 in the United States or 1.800.839.4769 in Canada.

NAVPRESS, the NAVPRESS logo, TH1NK, and the TH1NK logo are registered trademarks of NavPress. Absence of ® in connection with marks of NavPress or other parties does not indicate an absence of registration of those marks.

ISBN-13: 978-1-61747-899-4

Cover design by Arvid Wallen
Cover image by Shutterstock/Goodluz

Some of the anecdotal illustrations in this book are true to life and are included with the permission of the persons involved. All other illustrations are composites of real situations, and any resemblance to people living or dead is coincidental.

All Scripture quotations in this publication are taken from *THE MESSAGE* (MSG). Copyright © 1993, 1994, 1995, 1996, 2000, 2001, 2002. Used by permission of NavPress Publishing Group.

The grad's guide to healthy living : mind, body, soul, spirit / The Navigators.

    p. cm.

  Includes bibliographical references (p.   ).

  ISBN 978-1-61747-899-4

  1. High school graduates—Religious life. 2. High school graduates—Conduct of life.
3. College students—Religious life. 4. College students—Conduct of life.
5. Health—Religious aspects—Christianity. 6. Success—Religious aspects—Christianity.
I. Navigators (Religious organization)

  BV4531.3.G695 2012

  248.8'3—dc23

2011040786

Printed in the United States of America

1 2 3 4 5 6 7 8 / 17 16 15 14 13 12

Contents

INTRODUCTION

Congratulations—what an amazing achievement! The time and commitment required to graduate is no small thing, and hopefully you'll be able to look back at your time in high school and see how much you were able to accomplish by working hard.

And kudos to you for opening this book. You may have gotten it as a gift from someone who wants to give you as much information as possible before you head off to college. Maybe you're entering as a freshman, or maybe you're transferring after some time at a community college. Either way, the first time you move away is a big transition, even if it's just to a dorm room on campus.

This book will help you make that transition not only successful but also an amazing adventure. We've included some "Tips from the Trenches"—advice for you from current college students—that we hope you'll find helpful. Above all, this guide will give you a chance to think through some of the situations you'll encounter away from home so that you'll be ready when they come. Chances are you have some concerns already. Maybe you've never lived on your own. Maybe you're nervous about living with strangers. Maybe you're stressed about how to get involved in campus life.

Take a moment to grab a piece of paper and write down those things that are weighing on your mind. Sometimes just getting them out of your head can help you figure out what's really concerning you. Now tuck that paper into the back of this book. We'll look at it again when we're finished, and hopefully we'll have covered at least some of your concerns. If not, we'll have some more resources at the end of this guide for you to explore.

So what's this book about? Well, healthy living is something we all need to be concerned with. We have to take care of ourselves — body, mind, soul, and spirit — in order to do our very best at life. Now, some of you just saw the word spiritual and sighed or rolled your eyes. Yes, we'll be talking about your spiritual health, too, and that's because your physical and spiritual health are not only important but also intertwined. Paul talked about that physical/spiritual connection in 1 Corinthians 6:19-20:

> Didn't you realize that your body is a sacred place, the place of the Holy Spirit? Don't you see that you can't live however you please, squandering what God paid such a high price for? The physical part of you is not some piece of property belonging to the spiritual part of you. God owns the whole works. So let people see God in and through your body.

Regardless of where you'd put your spiritual health meter at the moment, you will find lots of useful information in here. So hang in there. And if your spiritual health is something that is already important to you, you'll find ways to maintain and even strengthen your walk with God while away at school.

God calls our body a "sacred place." The word *sacred* is interesting. Merriam-Webster calls it "dedicated or set apart for the service or worship of a deity."[1] From the outside in, we are meant to be set apart to serve God. Pretty heavy stuff.

What's even more interesting is what you'll find by looking back at when God explained to the Israelites how to build the temple in the wilderness. Chapter after chapter of Exodus is filled with details about curtain length, the materials they had to use, the number of rings and sockets and bars—exactly what everything should look like. God cared about every detail because it wasn't just a temple; it was the place where He would dwell.

Fast-forward a few thousand years and, because of Jesus' sacrifice, we are now the temple; God dwells within us through the Holy Spirit. Paul described it to the Ephesians like this:

> God is building a home. He's using us all — irrespective of how we got here — in what he is building. He used the apostles and the prophets for the foundation. Now he's using you, fitting you in brick by brick, stone by stone, with Christ Jesus as the cornerstone that holds all the parts together. We see it taking shape day after day — a holy temple built by God, all of us built into it, a temple in which God is quite at home. (Ephesians 2:19-22)

A temple where God can be at home. An amazing thought, isn't it? So with that in mind, do you think that the way we live and how we treat our bodies and hearts are important to the Lord? We think so too. So let's get ready to go to college!

1

The Magic Card

When arriving on campus, most students receive a "magic card." Usually it's just your campus I.D., but contained within its innocent magnetic strip is access to an endless amount of food choices all around campus. Your exact access will depend on what kind of dining plan you decided on, but even the humblest of plans can allow smorgasbord-level access to students.

Ever heard of the Freshman 15? Well, in case you've been too busy enjoying senior year, the Freshman 15 is the amount of weight the average freshman will gain during that first year away at school. It's not a myth that freshmen tend to gain weight, although the actual numbers vary quite widely. And it doesn't matter if you're a guy or a girl. The Freshman 15 comes simply from having unprecedented amounts of food to choose from and almost unlimited access to it at any time. On campus there most likely will be coffee stands, cafes, and other dining areas. You'll also probably find that the dining hall is open nearly all day long—breakfast, lunch, dinner, and sometimes even late at night — where you'll encounter various types of cuisine.

There's the pasta bar, with heaping pans of noodles and sauces. There are always slices of hot pizza to grab on your way out. And soda? Well, you're allowed to drink as much as you want (at 150 calories for every eight to twelve ounces). Then there's the hot food. And the cold food. There is even a salad bar, and you may think that's a safe place. But lurking at the salad bar are all sorts of rich dressings and sides, such as coleslaw and pasta salad. Even that three-bean salad has oils in it. And, of course, there's the dessert bar. Mom may not have given you dessert at every meal, but at college you can eat as much as you want.

Can you see where even the most health-conscious college student can get into trouble?

Taking Inventory

Before we dive in and deal with the magic card's access and all of the edible temptations college will have, let's see what your current eating habits are like.

Rate each question on a scale of 1 to 5:

> 1 (rarely) 2 (occasionally) 3 (sometimes)
> 4 (usually) 5 (most of the time)

____   1. I think about the food choices I make.

____   2. I eat fruits and vegetables every day.

____   3. I think about the portions of food I take in.

_____ 4. I try not to eat too much fast food.
_____ 5. I limit the amount of sweets I eat.
_____ 6. I eat the right amount of food (not too much, not too little).
_____ 7. I eat only when my body is hungry.
_____ 8. I make sure to get enough protein in my diet.
_____ 9. I limit the amount of junk food I eat.
_____ 10. I drink six to eight glasses of water each day.

Now simply add up the numbers and look at your total.

[40–50] You're doing great. You probably already think about the choices you make. Chances are that if you continue to do the same things in college, you can stay on track with a healthy diet.

[30–39] You're not completely unaware of what you're eating and drinking, but it sounds as though you may not always make the wisest choices for yourself. Look at the areas where you scored lower and keep an eye on those. Write down a goal or two for improving your score in those areas.

[29 or below] Well, my friend, you haven't given this area a ton of thought. And perhaps you haven't had to. But you'll want to be prepared for the changes ahead. You may even want to keep a food diary for a week or so to make yourself more aware of your eating habits.

The first step is always to be aware of how you eat and think about food because you will tend to do the same thing in college, only to a greater extreme. For example, if you tend to choose fried, fattier foods or have an insatiable sweet tooth now, those will be the same foods you will gravitate to at school. If you know what your weaknesses are, you can make a plan to avoid bad habits.

FROM THE TRENCHES

Stock up on nonperishable foods for your dorm. Many times the cafeteria gets repetitive.

Choosing Wisely

Whether you're already eating fairly healthfully or haven't thought about food at all, here are some basic tips to keep in mind when faced with the smorgasbord of choices available to you.

Color is always better. When filling your plate, see if there is color on it. If it tends to be only one basic color, that's a clue that you're not getting a variety of foods (specifically fruits and vegetables). No one is around to make you eat your vegetables anymore, so you'll need to start making those healthy choices on your own. Look for green leafy vegetables as well as other colors, like oranges, purples, and reds.

Try for five. During a given day, you should try to eat five servings of fruits and vegetables. If you want to get a more exact calculation of exactly how many fruits and vegetables you should be eating based on your age, gender, and activity level, visit the CDC website at www .fruitsandveggiesmatter.gov.

Find out how many fruits and veggies you should be eating.

Watch your portions. It's easy to pile it all on the plate without a thought. But the more you take means the more you're likely to eat. Make a fist and look at it. That's about the size of your stomach.[1] If you eat more than what your body needs, you will gain weight, so take small portions. If you're really still hungry, you can always go back for more.

Keep an eye on rich foods. The richer the food, the less you need of it to fill yourself up. Pasta, sauces, and foods that are cooked or soaked in oils tend to have far more calories. It doesn't mean you can't have them; it simply means you should take smaller portions and have those foods less often.

Variety is the spice of life. It's likely you already have your favorite foods, but be willing to try new things, especially foods that are heart healthy, such as fish. Branch out and try things you've never eaten before. Most households rotate through only eight staple meals, so there's a good chance you'll have the opportunity to try new and perhaps exotic dishes. You might be surprised at how much you enjoy them.

Beware of bread. Adding bread to every meal is usually unnecessary and packs on extra calories, so bypass the bread basket.

Navigate "dessert island" with care. Decide now that desserts can be enjoyed occasionally but not at every meal. Say no to them more often than you say yes. Dessert can be a great end-of-the-week reward.

FROM THE TRENCHES

Protein is a must for keeping your energy up. With a busy schedule, it's hard to squeeze in the right amounts of vitamins and minerals. Taco Bell is quick and easy, but too much fast food and junk food will take its toll. Try to make healthy choices.

Listening to Your Body 24/7

Food will be readily available to you. Not only can you find it in the dining halls and on-campus restaurants at your college, you'll even have food in your room, and takeout is just a phone call away. The eating behaviors of those around you will affect you as well. Maybe you have a roommate who likes to order pizza for his midnight study sessions. Or maybe someone on your hall is constantly baking cookies or making popcorn.

Before you grab that slice of pizza or that handful of popcorn, ask yourself if you're truly hungry. When your body needs fuel, it will let you know, but it's up to you to give your body the kind of fuel it needs. A pizza slice now and then isn't a big deal, but not giving your body a variety of nutritious foods can affect how you're feeling as a whole. Trust your body to let you know when you're hungry, and eat only when your body needs the fuel.

With everyone's schedule being different, you may also find yourself sitting down with a friend who needs to eat at a time when you may not. Don't eat just because someone else is eating. It's not rude. You can just grab a bottle of water and sip on that while you enjoy hanging out with your friends.

At the same time, you can't ignore your body's signals for food either. You may have a challenging class schedule or you find that you simply struggle to make time to sit down and eat right. In order for your body to perform at its optimum, you must give it the healthy food it needs.

Artificial Energy Versus Sustainable Energy

College students everywhere have to eat on the run sometimes, and it's tempting to grab coffee, high-sugar items such as cookies and doughnuts, or even energy drinks like Red Bull and Monster to keep yourself going. But sugar or caffeine-induced energy is really just artificial energy. The sugar crash that comes can hit you hard. And if you depend on sugar and caffeine to keep you going, the hard studying you do during that time isn't as effective as the studying that's done by someone who is eating and sleeping well.

It's like the difference between a runner who runs sprints and one who runs marathons. A sprinter must be able to perform at maximum energy for a short period of time, while a marathoner must be able to sustain energy over the long haul. College is a marathon. You can't sprint hard, crash, sprint hard, and crash again if you want to do well and make progress toward a career. If you choose to eat healthy foods on a regular basis, you'll find yourself more alert and able to adjust to the demands and pressures of college life. The bottom line is that your brain works better when you feed your body good things throughout the day.

FROM THE TRENCHES

You might not feel as though you have time to eat, but be sure you're getting enough good calories to sustain you. Skipping meals will significantly reduce the energy you'll have to do all the things going on throughout the day. Try packing a lunch the night before if the next day is going to be particularly busy.

Water Does a Body Good

If you're an athlete, you already know the importance of hydration, but the truth is that everyone needs to drink water every day. While water is contained in some of the foods we eat, drinking plain old water is still a necessity. You can use these tips to make sure you're staying hydrated.

Stay stocked. If you've got a refrigerator in your room, make sure you've always got cold water on hand. Whatever is easiest to grab is what you're most likely to drink.

Limit soda and coffee. If you don't tend to drink soda or coffee, don't start in college. If you enjoy them, make a deal with yourself to have no more than one per day (or one per week, if possible). You'd be surprised how quickly you can go through a six-pack of soda while you're studying for a statistics exam. Soda can really take a toll on your teeth and is full of empty calories. Limiting how much you drink can help protect you from weight gain. The key is being mindful about what you're drinking.

Carry a water bottle. One of the easiest ways to be sure to drink enough water is to simply carry a water bottle with you wherever you go. You can keep tabs on how much you're drinking by noting how often you refill the bottle throughout the day.

Planning for Success

We often have big ideas and grand plans, but putting them into action can be hit or miss. The more organized you are with your plans, the more likely you will be to stick to them. Take a few minutes to jot down the things that stuck out to you in this chapter. Maybe you rarely drink any water or maybe you tend to eat too much junk food. Whatever area you think you need to work on, write it down and then come up with a small achievable goal.

For example:

- Water—I will start drinking at least sixteen ounces of water per day.
- Fast food—I will eat fast food no more than once per week.
- Vegetables—I will make sure I eat at least one green vegetable every day.

Start small and work your way up. You can't expect to transform everything all at once, so give yourself the grace and time to get there, one step at a time.

2

Party All the Time?

No matter where you go to school—whether it's a small, private Christian college or a huge state university—there will be parties. Parties come in all shapes and sizes. Some are pretty safe and consist of a bunch of friends hanging out, listening to music, or watching a movie and generally just having fun. Others are not so safe.

Despite the fact that more than half of all college students are below the legal drinking age, alcohol is widely available to students across the nation. It's a given that it will be available, but what will you choose to do when it's offered to you? Sam's dorm at her university was considered "dry" (meaning no alcohol was allowed), yet keg parties occurred on the fifth floor nearly every weekend.

You may be reading this and thinking, *I don't go to parties; I don't plan to go to parties; there's nothing to see here.* Or maybe you're itching to get to college so that you can be free to do everything you're not allowed to do now. Most students are probably somewhere in between those two extremes. Let's take some time to look at the ways alcohol can affect you and your friends at school.

Legal Troubles

Possession of illegal substances (such as alcohol if you're under the age of twenty-one or drugs of any kind) can land you in trouble with the campus police as well as the local police. You risk probation or suspension on campus and any number of penalties in the locality of your college. The thing is, you don't actually have to have the substance yourself; if you're with someone who does, you could still end up with a battle to fight.

What if that person is a roommate? It could happen (and it's a terrible situation), but you'll have to be strong about the boundaries you set and what you're willing to have go on in your room. If you cannot work it out with your roommate, you may need to get help from your resident assistant (RA). It may even require moving to a different room. It's no fun to be a hostage to a living situation that not only makes you uncomfortable but also could land you in unnecessary legal trouble.

Academics

Using alcohol and drugs can seriously impact your academics. About 25 percent of college students report that drinking has had academic consequences.[1] Partying can cause you to be late for or miss classes, fall behind on studying, perform poorly on exams, and ultimately impact your grades. When you're paying as much as you are for school (and no matter where you go, your education is expensive), missing out on academics is costly.

Try out this math:

1. Find out what your tuition (plus the extra fees) is for the semester (or take your yearly tuition and divide it by 2).
2. Now divide that by 16. This gives you the amount your classes cost per week.
3. Divide that number by the number of credits you will take your first semester. (If you don't yet know how many credits you'll have, use 15 since that's a typical course load.)
4. Your answer is a rough estimate of what each hour of class costs.

To give you an idea, if your semester tuition is five thousand dollars and you take fifteen credits, every hour of class costs around twenty dollars. When you consider that it would take you more than forty hours of working at minimum wage to earn as much as one week of classes costs, you start to get an idea of the value of every hour of class you're paying for. Of course, this doesn't take into account room and board, which is also costing money. If you're interested, do the math using the full amount of your school, housing, and other related expenses and see what that number ends up being.

Now imagine you had to go pay that twenty dollars in cash whether you went to the class or not. You'll want to be sure you're making the most of every hour and minute you spend in the classroom. If you make the choice to party irresponsibly, it will impact your studies in one way or another because even if you show up to class, how clear-headed will you be if you're exhausted or hung over? Something to think about.

Death

We're not being overdramatic here; it's a simple fact that drinking excessive amounts of alcohol, driving under the influence of alcohol or drugs, or riding in a car with those who have consumed these substances can all result in injury or death. Getting in a car with someone who has been drinking even a little is a huge risk. Before you get in a car to go somewhere, you should make sure you have a safe way home. Plus, if you decide to drink as well, you risk not being able to make wise decisions about your health and safety. More about that later.

Alcohol Poisoning

It's important for you to recognize the signs of alcohol poisoning because even if you're not drinking, you will likely know people who are. Alcohol poisoning can kill someone quickly, so if you see even a few of the following signs, get help immediately by calling 911:

- Confusion, stupor
- Vomiting
- Seizures

- Slow breathing (less than eight breaths a minute)
- Irregular breathing (a gap of more than ten seconds between breaths)
- Blue-tinged skin or pale skin
- Low body temperature (hypothermia)
- Unconsciousness (passed out) and lacking the ability to be roused[2]

You can't worry about getting the person in trouble for being drunk when his or her life is at stake. If you see anyone exhibiting warning signs, get help immediately.

Drug Overdose

Drug overdoses are harder to pinpoint because a person's reaction depends on the kind of drug that was taken, and there are many different kinds. Unfortunately, you may not know that someone is in trouble until he or she actually loses consciousness. Treat it like any emergency:

1. Check for pulse and breathing.
2. Call 911.
3. Administer CPR if you are trained or instructed by the emergency operator. (It's an excellent idea for everyone to be trained in basic first aid and CPR.)

Some people are afraid to call for help, assuming that the person may just "sleep it off" or because of the belief or knowledge that they could get in trouble with the school or police. But over-doses of any kind are serious, and you won't necessarily be able to tell how serious it is from the outside. Trained professionals are the only ones able to accurately assess the health of someone who has possibly overdosed on drugs or alcohol.

Sex and Parties

Relationships with the opposite sex (something we'll talk about later) might be simply an issue of distraction, but adding alcohol or drugs to the mix can cause you to be in harm's way. Using alcohol or drugs of any kind and in any amount affects the way people think. Your mind is the control center of your whole body, so every decision you make is filtered through there. Alcohol and drugs make that control center malfunction, so regardless of where you stand on sexual activity in general, using alcohol or drugs increases the likelihood of having unprotected sex or being sexually assaulted.

It really doesn't matter how clear-headed or sure you are of what you will and will not do. Once you introduce alcohol and drugs into your body and brain, you'll lose control of your normal cognitive, reasoning, and decision-making skills. Even losing a little bit of that control can cause you to do things you would never normally do. Students under the influence of alcohol may not even know for sure if they consented to have sex. What's the most dangerous is losing all control, which is very easy to do, since you never know exactly how alcohol or drugs will affect you.

Leslie's Story

Leslie wasn't a drinker but went with her friends to a party, mostly because she knew that Kyle would be there. She spent some time during the party talking with him. He was drinking, although Leslie didn't know how much. It was clear that he was feeling pretty happy and invited her back to his room to talk where it was quieter. Leslie liked him. They were in a dorm, and she didn't feel unsafe, so Leslie went. But almost as soon as they got to the room, Kyle began to make sexual advances, at first just playfully. But the more she resisted, the more aggressive he became. He was bigger than her, stronger, and she struggled. She said no repeatedly, but she'd had enough alcohol to not remember for sure whether she'd used the word *help* — something that became pivotal during the trial.

She did eventually get free, and although she wasn't raped, the sexual assault shook her to her core. She struggled with the decision to report what happened because she blamed herself for going to the party, for drinking, and for willingly going to his room. The effects of the assault — the nightmares, the fear and anxiety — began to so affect her ability to continue at school that her friends eventually convinced Leslie to report the crime.

Because the assault occurred on campus, it was dealt with through the student court system and was a long, rather ugly, and dreadful process. Kyle adamantly denied any wrongdoing and insisted that Leslie was a willing participant. He had many friends testify in his defense. Leslie told her side of the story and also had many friends testify in her defense.

Kyle was kicked off campus but only for the rest of the school year. The next year, Leslie would occasionally see him on campus and continued to struggle with anxiety and depression over the event. No one makes their best decisions while under the influence. Perhaps Kyle would never have become so aggressive without the alcohol in his system. Perhaps Leslie wouldn't have gone to the dorm room. But this kind of incident (and incidents with much more dire and catastrophic results) is repeated on campuses all over the nation every year. Many sexual assaults go unreported for the very same reason that Leslie's almost did.

More help if you've been assaulted

You can't avoid every risky situation, but you can reduce your risk greatly by allowing your mind to be fully functional.

Get Moving!

Let's face it: You will spend a majority of your college career sitting on your bum, either in class or studying. If you live on a smaller campus, you may be walking between your classes, but campuses that are more spread out or in a city may require a bus to get around.

Unless you're naturally active and are the kind of person who joins a game no matter what everyone's playing, you'll want to find some time for exercise in your busy schedule. And like with most things in life, if you don't make a plan to do it, it might be easily pushed aside.

You don't have to exercise hours a day to receive the health benefits; just thirty minutes of focused exercise three days a week is all it takes. It does need to be focused, though. Walking to and from class throughout the day isn't the same as a brisk thirty-minute walk or jog.

Benefits of Exercise

Let's look at how exercise can actually help you while you're on campus.

Exercise improves your mood. Exercise produces chemicals in your body that help you feel more relaxed and happy. College can be a stressful place. Between navigating your studies and your relationships, you may find yourself feeling stressed out. Exercise can actually help you feel more confident and able to handle what's in front of you, and it's proven to help prevent and treat depression, too.[1]

Exercise helps control weight. Remember all that talk about the food that will be available to you 24/7? Well, building an exercise plan into your weekly schedule can help you feel healthier in general and keep you from gaining extra weight.

Exercise gives you energy. It might sound strange, but expending energy in quality exercise allows you to have more energy available to you. Imagine yourself sitting around your dorm room trying to finish studying for your statistics exam and you're falling asleep. Getting up and taking a walk will help clear your head better than trying to snag a ten-minute nap (unless it's three o'clock in the morning, in which case you should probably go to bed!).

Barriers to Exercising

Most of us know that exercise is good for our minds and bodies, but we can still neglect to do it if we're not focused on it. Even those who have been very active in high school can get to college and decide to take up other activities, not getting as much exercise as they used to. So what keeps us from exercising, and how can we overcome those obstacles?

Excuse #1 — Not enough time! Managing your time while on campus will be an ongoing challenge that changes with every class schedule and activity. But the truth is that if we think something is important and valuable, we'll make time to do it. A schedule or calendar — even if that's something you've never used before — will be very helpful in planning your time.

FROM THE TRENCHES

On your calendar or in your phone, block out time for your activities. Include your classes, meals, work schedule, time set aside for homework and friends, other tasks or errands you need to complete, and, of course, an exercise routine. You might want to create reminders on your computer or phone so you don't accidentally allow one activity to roll over into the time you set aside for something else.

Excuse #2 — It's boring! People who think exercise is boring just may not have found something they're interested in. Not all of us are created to love running or playing sports, but there are tons of other activities that will get you the exercise you need and may even be fun! Maybe you'd enjoy hiking on the weekends or trying your hand at rock climbing. College will offer you opportunities for activities that get your body moving in new ways.

Head over to the student life/activities center on campus or check bulletin boards for information about sports teams and clubs. Your academic advisor may also know whom you should talk to and where to find more information. Or take a look at the student activities page on your school website. You'll likely find more ways to stay fit than you even knew existed.

How to Get Exercise

On campus, there are a variety of ways to get the exercise you need. Let's explore some of the options. And although some of these naturally include more people (team sports, for instance), you can make any exercise more fun if you gather a group to work out with. If you love to do something, make signs and post them around campus to find other people who want to get exercise the same way. Not only will you find potential friends, you're more likely to stick with exercise if you have others joining you.

Running/jogging/walking. This is by far the easiest and most accessible form of exercise. And it may be something that works very well for you. Find a stretch of campus and just go for it. You don't need any special equipment, just a good pair of shoes and comfortable clothes. However, this kind of exercise also has a drawback: It's a bit weather dependent. You'll be far more likely to go for a walk or jog when the weather is nice, so you'll need to make a "bad weather plan" for when the conditions aren't right.

Go to the gym. Most campuses have a gym or recreation center that is available for your use. A gym can be an overwhelming place for the uninitiated, so if you're unfamiliar with working out in one, arm yourself with a plan. Many resources can be found online, but in general you'll want to do some cardiovascular exercise (on a treadmill, elliptical, stair climber, and so on) and some muscle strengthening (making sure to work different parts of your body). Keep in mind that sometimes when you get to the gym, the machines are occupied. Think of a backup plan. Jumping jacks or jumping rope can be a great substitute for cardiovascular exercise, and push-ups and crunches can fill the time as you wait for the machines to become available.

One resource that can help you plan your workout routine is SparkPeople. This free app allows you to track food and exercise and also helps you build an exercise plan to use in a gym.

Download the app.

Your campus gym may also offer various workout classes or have places where you can swim and play racquetball, tennis, or basketball. Grab some other people and play!

Join a team. Playing on your college sports team may not be an option for you, especially if you go to a Division I school, but nearly every campus has intramural (or club) sports where students get together to have fun playing. Most of the time, intramural sports allow everyone to participate, so if you've always wanted to try a sport, it's not too late! Take a look at your school's website or athletic department to find out more about the teams. If you're looking for something more competitive, check out club sports, which usually place a high degree of emphasis on student organization, management, and initiative.

Create a club. Want to do a yoga or Pilates class but can't find anywhere to take one? Want to play a sport that's not listed at your college? Well, you can step up and create clubs or classes on your own. Check with the student life or athletic department to find out about the process. You never know: There may be a bunch of other students who'd love to participate as well!

But you don't have to have a formal club to get some people together to work out. Whatever it is you love to do, chances are there are others out there just like you. Maybe you can start an exercise class right in your own dorm. It doesn't have to be complicated. Pop a DVD into a laptop, move the furniture aside, and just go for it. Love to play Frisbee? Put up some flyers in the dorms and have an informal game on one of the lawns.

Audit a class. Many colleges allow students to take a class without receiving formal credit. This way, you can participate without having to worry about a grade that could affect your GPA. You could take a variety of health and exercise classes that way. If your school has a dance department, taking a dance class can also be a fun way to stay in shape. Join a weightlifting class to learn more about your muscles and how to stay fit. Work on the backstage crew at your theater department by building and moving sets. There are lots of options!

Your Exercise Plan

Just like with food, variety is best. You'll probably get bored and stop your routine if you have only one basic plan. Start by deciding how often you want to work out. Three days a week is a great place to begin. While you may want to do more, having a minimum goal to shoot for is usually more manageable. Developing an exercise plan is easier if you start to get a sense for what will work for you. Answer the following questions to help you begin developing your exercise plan:

- How many days a week do I want to get some exercise?
- What are five types of exercise that are most interesting to me?
- Do I prefer working out alone, or do I like to be with a group?
- What are some clubs or groups I'd like to look for on campus?
- What are some obstacles I might face in getting regular exercise?
- What can I do to deal with the obstacles?
- What can I do to make exercise a part of my overall health plan?

Using your answers to these questions, pick three activities that you think you can reasonably fit into your schedule on a regular basis. Remember to keep your goals manageable by choosing a minimum amount, such as thirty minutes three times a week. If you get the chance to do a lot more, that's great; if not, you've gotten in enough to keep your body healthy.

How to start an exercise program

A Time for Everything

Ecclesiastes talks about there being a time for everything under the sun. Exercise is a component of healthy living, but just like everything else we're talking about, moderation is the key. Get some regular exercise, but don't make it more important than everything else. Some people can take exercise to levels that become unhealthy. That's why college can be such a big transition. There are so many things pulling for your time and attention that it's easy to get out of balance. We'll talk more in a later chapter about how you can recognize problems that may occur with yourself or others.

4

Sweet Sleep

With so much going on at school, sleep is about the last thing some college students worry about. There's a reason the term *all-nighter* originates with students staying up all night to complete schoolwork or prepare for an exam. But sleep is as important as healthy eating habits and exercise. Most Americans don't get enough sleep in general, so you can imagine how that extends to students who have classes and countless other activities.

The average student is between eighteen and twenty-four years of age, and the National Sleep Foundation (yes, a whole foundation devoted to encouraging people to get the sleep they need!) recommends seven to nine hours a night for adults. If you're on the younger end, you may actually need an extra hour. If you consistently get less than that, sleep deprivation (or sleep debt) can begin. Sleep deprivation, even in smaller doses, can be serious business.

Who Needs Sleep Anyway?

Everyone! Even the Bible talks about sleep. Proverbs 3:24 speaks of how our sleep can be sweet. Solomon writes in Ecclesiastes 5:12 of how someone who labors well will rest better than a rich man. And in Isaiah 50:11, we learn that sleep can be tormented. Having trouble sleeping can be a symptom of a deeper spiritual condition. When we can't settle our minds enough to sleep well, there may be issues of concern we're not handling well. We'll talk about our spiritual health in chapter 11, but if you're having trouble with sleep, the best place to start is to take a look at where you're at spiritually.

We spend a good portion of our lives asleep, and it helps us in so many ways. We were designed by God to need rest, and we can push our bodies and minds only so far before they simply cannot do anymore without the proper sleep. Let's look at some of the benefits of getting enough quality sleep.

Stay healthy. The less sleep you get, the less robust your immune system will be. Your body will be exposed to all sorts of viruses and bacteria when you live with other people, so the stronger your immune system, the more able you are to fight off illness when it comes your way.

Think better. The better you sleep, the better you think. College is an intense academic experience, so you'll want all of your mental faculties to be as sharp as possible. Remember how they told you before the SATs to get a good night's sleep and eat a good breakfast in the morning? Well, that pretty much applies to college in general.

Wake up more easily. If you don't get enough sleep, your body will struggle to wake up. Frequently, that can cause a caffeine cycle. You get to bed late, you get up early for class, you drink caffeine to keep yourself awake, and then you struggle to get to sleep again. That damaging pattern can be repeated over and over. The other issue is that if you're struggling to wake up, you may decide to skip classes in order to get the sleep you need. That also can become a bad pattern if you're not careful.

Making Your Sleep Better

College presents a whole new set of challenges when it comes to rest. Stress or worry can make it hard to fall asleep even if you're tired. Here are some tips when it comes to trying to get a good night's rest.

Use your bed only for sleeping. In a dorm room or apartment, it's easy to use your bed for everything from eating your dinner to studying to just staying up late talking. But you can teach your body to be more receptive to sleep by settling into bed only when it's time to sleep. It seems like a small thing, but it can be really helpful, especially if you struggle occasionally with insomnia.

Watch your caffeine intake. You may be one of those people who swears that caffeine doesn't affect them, but as you get into the college years, your body might begin to respond differently. Whereas a Dr Pepper before bed may not have bothered you as a freshman in high school, it might keep you from settling down when you're a freshman in college. Try not to have any caffeine past 5 p.m. and you'll likely find that your body will be more settled and able to sleep.

Be prepared for your roommates. An early bird and a night owl sometimes get thrown into the same room together, making for a rather uncomfortable situation at times. Whether you are the night owl who avoids eight o'clock classes like the flu, or the early bird who thinks sleeping past sunrise is a waste, you'll want to be prepared on either end. When you come to college, make sure you have:

- An eye mask
- Earplugs
- An alarm clock (Consider one that will vibrate so it can wake you without disturbing your roommate, but test it on a weekend before you rely on it to wake you up for your first class.)

You'll be glad to have these items in case your roommate has a strange habit of tapping his foot on the floor while he's studying late at night or she can't seem to dress in the morning without slamming every drawer and door in the room.

Create consistent sleep patterns. Try, as much as you are able, to go to bed at the same time and wake up around the same time each day. This kind of schedule can be hard to maintain, but if you help your body get into a consistent rhythm, you'll sleep more soundly and feel more rested. There will be times when you'll need to go to bed later or wake up earlier, but if you are generally consistent, it will help a great deal in giving you the rest you need.

TIP

FROM THE TRENCHES

Get sleep. Make sure you use your time wisely enough so that you can get enough sleep. Your body might be able to take a few nights on little to no sleep, but it wears on you quickly, and the last thing you need is to be getting sick in the busiest part of the semester.

Risky Business

We've already talked a little about the party atmosphere that exists at most colleges in some form or another. A college student I met the other day said that she's been frustrated with some of the students in her department because they aren't serious about learning and working. Instead, they just want to party all the time. You might be thinking this only happens at some schools or that by attending a Christian college, you won't encounter people like this, but the problem isn't restricted to secular campuses. Anywhere you go, there will be some who don't really care about getting a decent education and are instead focused on their next social event.

The people around you will offer temptations and influences, both good and bad. This is why thinking through your own priorities before you go away to school can be so valuable. How will you respond when a bunch of your friends decide to go to a party and you've got a biology exam to study for?

While we've already discussed alcohol and drugs and how the use of those substances can make the possibility of sexual assault and rape more real, we haven't really talked about how college will introduce you to a whole range of ideas about sex.

The Guttmacher Institute has found that by their nineteenth birthday, seven out of ten men and women have had sex.[1] That's right in the middle of the college years, so that kind of leads to the next question.

Where Do You Stand on Sex?

Before we go any further, let's take a short inventory about your ideas and thoughts about sex. Not your parents' ideas. Not your church's ideas. Not your friends'. What *you* think. What *you* believe to be true. Because these are ideas, they should be in your own words. Take a few minutes to come up with ten statements about sex and what you believe to be true. You may have to really think about it, but if you take a bit of time to truly ponder, you'll find that your thoughts will start to form. If you're struggling, here are some open-ended sentences to help you get started.

I believe that sex is _____.

Sex is meant to be _____.

I will have sex when _____.

My concern about sex is _____.

I want to have sex when _____.

The reason it's important to think through your ideas is because statistically you will make a decision to either have sex or not have sex during your college years. That might be because you find yourself in a committed relationship, possibly for the first time. Your partner's ideas about sex will also play into your decision. You may feel pressure one way or another by the other person's thoughts and beliefs. If you know what you believe before you're in a sexual situation, you're more likely to stick to your resolutions.

What Is God's Opinion About Sex?

While we could spend the next few pages recounting every Scripture and make statements about those Scriptures, it may not really make a difference. You might think you've heard it all before and just skip those sections. Some of you may not be sure where you stand with God or what He might think about sex. But here's the thing: God does have an opinion on sex. After all, He created it. How can you find out what He has to say about it?

Study the Scriptures with an open mind. It's important to not approach the Bible trying to prove you're right, because you will surely find something in there that justifies what you believe, even if you're wrong. The attitude of our heart is important. Are you willing to discover what God really has to say about the topic? Are you willing to hear things that might challenge what you think you believe?

As you study Scripture about God's plan for sex and sexuality, be sure to read the whole passage, not just a single verse. Sometimes reading the surrounding verses (and even chapters) can give you more insight into the meaning of a particular verse. Understanding the context is important anytime you study Scripture.

Pray for wisdom. The Scriptures tell us that if any of us lack wisdom, we should ask God for it. Ask Him to show you His truth. Ask Him to speak to your heart and give you wisdom about the topic. Ask Him to help you not have an agenda but rather be open to listening to Him.

Use a concordance to look up *sex, sexual relations, intercourse*, and other variations of these words. A concordance gives you a list of every Scripture a certain word appears in. There are several online concordances, some of which give you the same Scripture in different translations. These can be very helpful. Keep in mind that different Bible translations might use different words. An online concordance will likely offer the most verses related to the words you look up. Try looking up the same passage in different translations so you can gain a better understanding.

Interact and ponder. While you are studying the Scriptures, use a notebook or journal to record what you're noticing about the things you're reading. What stands out to you? Here's a list of questions that can help you think about the words:

- What is something you learned?
- What stood out to you?
- Did something confuse or surprise you?
- How can what you read help you in your life?
- What do you learn about God (or what He thinks) in this passage?

Think of the Bible like a mirror. In the morning, when you're getting ready to go out, you don't just take a quick glance in the mirror and run off. (Well, we've all done that at times probably, but it's not the norm. Usually, we spend a bit of time checking out our reflections, fixing our hair and faces, checking our teeth, and so on.) If you take a quick glance at the Bible and then run away, you're missing out on the chance to see what God might want to show you.

Journaling is a great way to think about what you've read before you run off. Take some time to record what you're seeing, to be honest about your questions, and to learn what God has to say, especially about the topic of sex. Once you've had a chance to do this, see if you can write down ten things the Bible says about sex. Here are a few open-ended statements to get you going. Spend some time with this. Try not to let your own opinions stop you from writing down what you see in the Word.

The Bible says sex is _____.

Sex is meant to be _____.

The purpose of sex is _____.

Sex should occur _____.

Now compare the two sets of statements — your first set of beliefs (from page 44) and what you believe you see in the Scriptures. Are there things in common? Where do the lists differ? Will you make your decision based on what *you* think or what *God* says?

What Do You Believe?

When it comes to making daily decisions, especially while you're away at school, what you really believe plays a big role in how you make those decisions. By thinking these things through before you go away, you'll be more prepared when situations arise that demand a decision.

We live in a media culture right now in which teens and young adults in movies and on television sleep around with multiple partners, have casual sex with people they don't know well (hookups at parties), and have "friends with benefits." You will run into a wide range of people with a wide range of beliefs, from those who view sex as simply a "fun activity" to those who view it as meant for only those in a committed marriage.

 FROM THE TRENCHES

Ignore peer pressure and gossip. Don't let the people around you change who you are. College is a totally different environment from high school. You will be pressured from all sides. Find friends who will be good influences instead of the reverse.

The Risk of Sex

Those who choose to be sexually active automatically inherit a number of risks. Sex is more than just a moral decision; it's a decision that can affect your physical and mental health as well. First, let's take a look at the physical realities of sexual activity.

Pregnancy

Sex makes babies; it's as simple as that. And if you're headed off to college, you already know that. But when you are in a sexually charged situation, it's easy to forget that sex is meant to provide a way to create new life. It's truly an amazing creative process that was designed by God. But when you are seventeen, nineteen, or even twenty-one, a baby is probably not in your plans. Yes, contraception is widely available and, yes, it can reduce the chance of getting pregnant, but if you choose to have sex, there will always be a very real chance of pregnancy.

Every teen who has gotten pregnant or gotten someone pregnant thinks it can never happen to him or her. But if you consider yourself responsible and mature enough to choose to have sex, you are also committing to the reality that you could become pregnant or get someone pregnant. If you don't want to start a family right now in your life, having sex is a very risky choice.

Multiple Partners

It's not uncommon for college students to go through a number of relationships as they figure out what matters to them and who they are becoming. But if those college students are sleeping with everyone they date, they could be racking up a large list of partners, which greatly increases the risk of sexually transmitted infections.

Sexually Transmitted Infections (STIs)

While pregnancy is a real possibility, young adults are even more likely to contract a sexually transmitted infection. You've probably heard the idea that if you choose to have sex with someone, you are choosing to have sex with everyone they've had sex with. It is true. You have no way of knowing for sure the sexual history of one person, much less the sexual history of everyone he or she has ever slept with. And you don't have to actually have intercourse to expose yourself to disease. Additionally, some of these infections can render you infertile or make getting pregnant very difficult. If you ever want to have a family, these infections are very risky. Let's look at some of the most common infections:[2]

Crabs. These are parasitic lice that live in the pubic region. This infection is more of a nuisance with such symptoms as itchiness, fevers, and tiredness. This is one infection that is curable, but you'll still need to see a doctor for a prescription medication.

Chlamydia. Initially, chlamydia presents a lot like a yeast or bladder infection, but this is far more serious. If left untreated, this infection can spread into your uterus and pelvis, causing pelvic inflammatory disease (PID). PID can leave a woman with chronic pelvic pain as well as the risk of ectopic pregnancy (when a baby develops in the fallopian tube rather than in the uterus) and infertility. The scary thing about this one is that the infection can spread into the pelvis even when there are no symptoms. Because many of the common symptoms resemble flu symptoms (nausea, fever, and pain in the lower back and abdomen), many people don't discover the infection until it's already spread. And when men carry the infection, they sometimes don't have symptoms at all, so they continue to spread it without knowing it.

Experts estimate there are 2.8 million *new* infections per year, and even though you can treat chlamydia,[3] many don't even know they have it, so they don't pursue treatment and continue to spread it to new partners.

Genital herpes. Usually, people do not know they have genital herpes until the blisters appear (and those without blisters may not know they're infected). Symptoms include painful red bumps or blisters in the genital region accompanied with pain and discomfort, fever, headaches, and muscle soreness. The symptoms can subside after two to four weeks and then return later for another episode, year after year. Although there may be times when the infected person experiences no symptoms and has no visible blisters, the infection can be passed on in between breakouts. This infection can also be passed from a mother to a child during birth, so carrying this infection poses serious risks to a newborn, including death. Though medication can be used to help manage the symptoms of genital herpes, there is no cure for the infection.

Gonorrhea. Many people do not realize they have this infection either, and it can often be mistaken for a bladder or yeast infection. It can cause discharge, pain, and soreness. If it's left untreated it can spread into the pelvis and cause PID. This infection is treatable but can have long-term consequences, including infertility. The challenge is receiving treatment quickly enough when you may or may not have symptoms.

Hepatitis B. Hepatitis B is an infection that attacks the liver. It can cause such symptoms as yellowish skin, tiredness, nausea, vomiting, diarrhea, joint pain, and abdominal pain, but someone carrying Hepatitis B may not have any symptoms at all. Many people are given vaccines to try to prevent this particular disease.

Hepatitis C. This infection presents a lot like the Hepatitis B infection and also attacks the liver. It can cause tiredness, yellowing of the skin and eyes, abdominal pain, and loss of appetite. There is no cure for this infection, but it can be managed with prescription medications. Eight out of ten people who carry this infection do not have symptoms, so it can be passed on easily.

HIV/AIDS. HIV stands for human immunodeficiency virus. It attacks the immune system of your body. Although this particular sexually transmitted disease is thought by many to be under control and primarily limited to homosexual relationships, that's just not the case. Young people are still actively contracting and spreading this disease, and 34 percent of new cases are among heterosexuals. According to the Centers for Disease Control, having another STI can increase your risk of contracting or transmitting HIV.[4] Here again, symptoms might not be present, so it's possible to unknowingly spread or be exposed to the disease.

HIV has a terrible set of symptoms, and they might not appear until years after exposure. Symptoms include extreme tiredness, weight loss, frequent low fevers and night sweats, frequent infections or contraction of other STIs, and skin markings. Thanks to new medications, people are living longer with the disease, but the medications have very unpleasant side effects and the disease can still lead to AIDS.

AIDS stands for acquired immune deficiency syndrome. It is usually diagnosed when your body has contracted certain infections or cancers caused by the damage done by HIV to your body's immune system. Acquiring HIV or AIDS can lead to an increased risk of premature death, especially if left untreated.[5]

Human papillomavirus (genital HPV). Most do not know they are infected with this, but if there are symptoms, they can include genital warts and cell changes on the cervix with women. These cell changes can lead to cervical cancer over time. The conditions HPV causes can be treated with medication and proper screenings to check for cancer growth, but there is no treatment for HPV itself.

Syphilis. There are two distinct stages to this infection. The first usually consists of sores in the genital region and swollen lymph glands that heal on their own in about three to six weeks. If treatment does not begin during the early stages of the infection, it can progress to worsening symptoms such as rashes, fevers, hair loss, sore throat, tiredness, and weight loss. Syphilis can eventually cause nerve and brain damage as well as death if not treated.

What should you do if you suspect you may have already been exposed to an STI? In every case, you'll need to see a doctor for the proper treatment since all of the infections we've mentioned require monitoring and most likely prescription-strength medications. Managing any kind of

STI fact sheets

infection on your own increases the risk that damage could be done to your health and reproductive organs.

Worth the Risk?

Basically, many of the worst infections can unknowingly be carried by someone and given to their partner, so someone telling you they're healthy means very little. They might not even know what's going on inside of them. And some of these diseases can be contracted simply through sexual contact—not necessarily intercourse—so even "fooling around" may have exposed you or a partner to many of these infections.

And while some of these infections are treatable, many of them have no cure. That means you will have to deal with it in some form or another for the rest of your life. Add that to the risk of infertility or passing the infection on to a baby and you have to ask yourself, *Is the temporary pleasure of sex worth the long-term risks I am taking?*

College is a time of growth in so many ways. During this time, you'll be figuring out a lot about yourself and what you want out of your future. Complicating your emotional health and risking your physical health with sexual relationships is a pressure you can choose to avoid altogether.

Your Future Mate

One day you'll need to share your sexual history with someone you deeply love and want to marry and spend the rest of your life with. Before you make a sexual decision, think about having to tell your future mate about the experience and the potential effect it may have on your relationship.

Pornography

For a long time, pornography has been considered a "guys' problem," but women are increasingly admitting to the same struggles in this area as men. With movies and TV shows that have highly sexualized content, and the ready availability of porn over the Internet, dealing with porn is an issue you may run across during college.

Pornography is addictive. Men and women suffer very real damage from the effects of pornography, within themselves as well as in their relationships. Frequently used a lot like alcohol or any other drug that stimulates the senses, pornography is highly addictive, which is why it is a temptation best avoided. Because of porn's addictive nature, those who use it will tend to slowly escalate the types of porn they use in order to receive the same high.

Pornography damages relationships. Pornography can create and fuel sexual desires to such a degree that sexual relationships become a primary concern and emotional relationships can be ignored. The fantasy world it creates in the mind of the viewer is ultimately false and can destroy real intimacy with someone. While popular culture can sometimes turn a blind eye to the use of porn and its effects, pornography does damage to relationships, leading to secrecy, unrealistic expectations, and insecurity.

Pornography has a spiritual impact. Pornography use of any kind can damage our spiritual walks and greatly reduce our ability to connect with God and others. Typically, Christians who struggle in this area feel a deep sense of shame because they often know that what they're doing is wrong. Frequently, they create a hidden self so they can indulge in their

XXXchurch.com offers help and resources.

sin but then present themselves as something else in front of others.

Sexting

When phones became capable of taking pictures and sending them, the advent of a newer form of pornography occurred. Sexting is when one person takes a nude or partially nude picture of themselves or others and sends it to someone else.

The issues with this are many. Even if you right now can't even imagine the idea that someone would ask you to take such a picture, it could happen. And the fact is, you may even be tempted to do it, especially if it's someone you really like. But it's not a sign of love or interest; it's a huge flashing neon sign of disrespect. It's not flirting. It's not innocent. It's a violation of your privacy that someone doesn't have a right to ask for or access.

And perhaps you know that and would be quick to say no and realize what kind of person would suggest it. But your roommate or someone down the hall may be more unsuspecting. Understanding what could happen allows you to be ready when you encounter it yourself or if you have a friend who gets into a tough situation.

One of the risks of sexting is the likelihood that a private picture will become public. You may think the person receiving the picture would never show anyone else, but ponder some of the possibilities. What happens if after a bad breakup your ex sends your picture to others? Who might those people send it to next? Another risk you might take is a legal one. What happens if someone presses charges? What happens if you or another person involved is under age eighteen? Possessing a pornographic picture from or sending it to someone younger than eighteen is punishable by law.

Party Pictures

You'll want to be cautious of the kinds of pictures that are taken of you and can easily end up on the Internet, even pictures in which you're clothed. Do you want a potential employer to discover online pictures of you partying in college? Nowadays, a picture can be snapped and uploaded to the Internet not only within an instant but with information about your whereabouts for anyone to see. In general, you'll want the person on the other side of the camera to be someone you trust. Even then, be careful about what you do in pictures. Sometimes something innocent can appear to be something else in a picture.

Wise as a Serpent, Gentle as a Dove

More than anything, you'll need to develop a discerning spirit when it comes to the people you are around. You have to be smart and wise and very careful about whom you choose to trust. We don't like to think about how many awful people are out there, but the truth is that there are many who will actively deceive you for one reason or another. Some people will say absolutely anything to get you to do what they want you to do, and that includes trying to convince you to have sex. And this isn't just for the girls; guys can be deceived too. Keep an eye out for red flags concerning others' behavior:

- Lying to you or others
- Overdone flattery
- Substance abuse of any kind

- Elaborate stories designed to make you feel sorry for them
- Exaggeration (making them look like someone they're not)
- Arrogance
- Jealousy or possessiveness
- Trying to control what you do, where you go, and whom you spend time with
- Anger issues
- Neediness (creating ways to get your attention)

As a college student, you should never be called upon to be more than just a supportive and listening friend. If you feel that someone has issues, you're probably right. But the best thing you can do for someone is encourage him or her to get some help (see chapter 9 or the resources section).

The Emotional Side of Sex

We've talked about a number of the risks associated with having sex, but one of the biggest is much harder to categorize: the risk to your heart. Sex was designed to be a deeply intimate connection between two people fully committed to each other in marriage. When you have sex, you open yourself emotionally to someone in deep ways you may not even understand at the time. If the relationship ends, not only do you have the pain that goes along with any breakup but the person also takes with him or her that gift of intimacy and love you gave away. It can hurt, and it can have lasting effects, sometimes leading to fear of being hurt again or distrust of people. You might even feel the effects in your relationship with your wife or husband.

You're worth more than the negative effects — physical, spiritual, and emotional — of a sexual relationship that doesn't fulfill God's beautiful purpose for sex.

Staying Safe On Campus

Every college and university takes the safety of its students very seriously. They want you to be able to come to the school and learn and grow in a safe environment. Each campus has its own set of safety measures that have been put in place, and each year, changes are made to improve the safety systems.

When you arrive on campus for orientation, the leaders will share with you their campus system and how to access the help you need. Take this seriously. You know how on a plane hardly anyone listens to the safety procedures? We think we know it all, but in an emergency situation, our ability to remember information is put under tremendous pressure, so we tend to go by instinct. You'll want to pay close attention to how to access help at your school, from non-emergency help to reporting problems to dealing with sudden emergencies.

If your school provides an emergency help sheet that quickly explains the procedures, be sure to post it in your room as a reminder.

If not, you can make your own sheet with the basics. It may sound a little lame, but the more familiar you are with your campus, the safer you'll be.

Many schools have implemented a text-message system for campus-wide alerts. This is one of the positive things that came out of the Virginia Tech massacre, one of the worst college campus tragedies. A student killed thirty-two people on April 16, 2007. It was a devastating event, not only for the families of those who lost loved ones but also for the entire community of Virginia Tech. The massacre began when a lone gunman, a student at the school, shot two other students in a residence hall that he was not supposed to have access to. Then nearly two hours later, and after mailing a manifesto and self-made videotapes to NBC news, the gunman entered one of the academic buildings and chained the doors shut. He began shooting in multiple classrooms, and when he killed himself, thirty-two people were dead and many were injured.

The event itself would be tragedy enough, but it raised concerns about the safety of every student on every campus around the nation. How can we make campuses safe? What failed? How can we prevent something like this from happening again? Those were the questions Virginia Tech and every other college faced.

A special panel was appointed by the governor of Virginia to look into the tragedy, and they learned a lot from what had happened. Many changes were instituted, not just in Virginia but across the nation. Let's look at the lessons they learned that would impact you as you go away to school.

Alert Systems

When the Virginia Tech massacre happened, students were warned and notified of the danger on campus through e-mails. The problem was that many students never received those e-mails because they were away from their computers or sitting in class. The need for campus-wide instant-alert systems was clear, and most colleges now have some kind of alert system in place. That's why it's important to know exactly how your school will communicate with you. Some schools will need you to register your phone number in order to receive text alerts, and although you may not want to give your phone number out, opting into the alert system is the safer choice. And even though you might occasionally get "false alarm" alerts, try to take them seriously.

Access

Someone let the gunman into that dorm, and it was probably such a simple little thing that no one thought anything about it. Ever held the door open for someone? That's pretty much all it would've taken for the gunman to get past the security-card system used by that campus dorm. Your residence hall will have safety procedures in place, and they can occasionally seem silly, but everyone is safer if you follow the rules. So even if someone calls you a jerk for not letting them into your building (even if you've seen them around before), you just never know when you might actually be saving someone's life.

Early Warning Signs

Before the shooting, the gunman had several incidents occur that were clear warnings of mental instability. Several people reported different incidents, but no one really connected the dots of what was going on with this young man. The lesson you can take away is that if you believe another student to be troubled, unstable, or even dangerous, reporting it is the only way to help keep everyone safe. If someone is making either direct or indirect threats of any kind, that should also be reported. In this case, the cliché is true: better to be safe than sorry.

Hopefully this is something you will never have to face. But sometimes the unimaginable does happen, and you can be prepared. Stay alert to your surroundings. Make sure you know how your campus handles emergencies, everything from shootings to such weather emergencies as tornadoes. Verify that you're signed up to receive text-message alerts if that's something your school offers. Be involved in the safety of your community.

How to Stay Safe

While most young women know they need to stay alert to be safe, young men shouldn't take their safety for granted either. Crimes against men — beatings, robberies, and assaults — can happen. College is very much a community, and as a member of the community, you can help the campus stay safer. The first thing to do is use the systems put in place already. If your school has a way to ensure your safe return from parking lots late at night, use it. If you are able to call for a free ride home, use it. Don't assume you'll be fine.

Know the School

Where are the alert boxes on your campus? How will the school alert you if there is an emergency? How late can you stay in your favorite study spot and still get back to your dorm safely? What's the safest way to get from class to class? What paths are lighted? What paths should be avoided at night? All of these questions are ones you'll be able to answer if you really pay attention in orientation and are aware of your surroundings. Don't be afraid to ask questions and get tips from those who have been on the campus for more than a year.

Use a Buddy System

Don't travel alone if at all possible. Walk with others and you'll not only squeeze in time to enjoy friends, you'll also be safer. This is especially true for jogging. You can probably run safely by yourself in heavily traveled, well-lighted areas of your campus, but if you're going to venture out even a little bit, find a running partner and commit yourself to not taking a risk. There have been countless assaults and kidnappings that have occurred when a runner has been out alone.

Report Suspicious Behavior

It can be hard to report people who are actually part of your campus community, but if their behavior is suspicious or threatening, you are helping keep others safe by letting someone in authority know of your concern. Let the police sort out whether there is something to worry about or not.

Communicate

It's a good idea to be aware of your friends' and roommates' schedules. It's possible that your best bud is someone other than your roommate, but your roommate should still know what your schedule is each semester. Exchange copies of your class and work schedules. That way, if there is a problem, someone knows how to get ahold of you or knows when something might be terribly wrong.

When you head out, be sure someone—your roommate, a friend, or someone on your floor—knows where you are and when you're planning to come back. You can leave a handwritten note, text someone, or write it on the bathroom mirror, but let someone know.

Rape

While some of the guys may want to tune out right about now, rape is a topic that anyone living on a college campus needs to be aware of. With one in four women being sexually assaulted, you will likely know someone who has been affected by rape. And in truth, it's also possible for men to be raped or assaulted.[1] The statistics are rather staggering:

- The highest risk of a woman being raped is between the ages of twelve and thirty-four.

- Two-thirds (66 percent) of assaults are committed by someone known to the victim, and 38 percent of rapists are a friend or acquaintance.
- Sixty percent of rapes and sexual assaults go unreported.[2]

How to Avoid Rape

Your best defense is your own discernment about people. Given that most rapes and sexual assaults are committed by people the victim knows, it stands to reason to not blindly trust someone just because you know who he or she is.

By doing some of the things we've already talked about—not using substances, staying with a buddy, and avoiding situations where you'll be alone with someone—you can reduce your risk. Unfortunately, there are no guarantees that something won't happen. We live in a world where evil is very present, and while you can be smart and make wise choices, bad things can still happen to you or someone you know.

What to Do If It Happens to You

Being sexually assaulted can make someone instinctively do things that might reduce the person's chances of getting justice, such as taking a shower, not wanting to talk to anyone, or not reporting what happened. If the unthinkable occurs:

- Do not shower.
- Call a rape crisis hotline (1-800-656-HOPE). The counselors know how to help you or your friend, and they'll walk with you every step of the way.

- Go to the emergency room. It may be difficult to do this or to convince a friend to go, but it's important to get physically checked out and allow the hospital staff to collect any evidence left behind by the attack.
- Get tested. The ER will likely run initial tests, but after six months and a year, you'll want to get retested to make sure you haven't been exposed to any STIs.
- Get support. Find someone to talk to, someone you can trust.
- Get into counseling. Any kind of assault can be difficult to process, and the emotional fallout will take longer to heal than the physical fallout. Most campuses have some sort of department that can help, or your local rape crisis center may be able to recommend some counselors who are experienced with sexual assault victims. This step is absolutely critical.
- Give yourself time. Like any traumatic event, it will take time to heal. Give yourself the freedom to grieve. But at the same time, pursue healing and forgiveness, for your own sake.

More help if you've
been assaulted

Predators

Predators are called predators for a reason. There are those who will lie in wait and grab someone who decides to go running in a dark park alone at night, and there are other types of predators who are far more calculating. They watch your habits, they watch what you do, they may even reach out and try to befriend you, all the while planning to do you harm. It stinks that we live in a world like this, but we still need to be ready for it, and this is true for everyone, not just college students!

The more available you make your personal information and habits to strangers, the more at risk you put yourself. In general, you simply want to make yourself less of a target. You can do that in several ways:

- Don't travel alone.
- Don't use substances that will impair your judgment in any way.
- Don't allow anyone you don't know to access your personal information and photos.
- Be aware of your surroundings.
- Don't agree to meet with someone you "met" online.
- Report and block anyone who makes you uncomfortable.

It's never a good idea to communicate with or establish any kind of relationship with someone you met online. You have tons of real-life possibilities right there on your campus, so don't get sidetracked with people who may not be who they say they are or could even be downright dangerous to you. It's not worth the risk.

Online Safety

You probably think you've heard it all when it comes to online safety, but stay with us. Up until now, you've been dealing with a different kind of community at home, and now you will be on a campus. Some of the ways to stay safe are ones you may have heard, but we'll look at it specifically from the aspect of someone living on campus. Here are some general tips for staying safe online:

- Be sure your phone number is not listed, and never post it where others can see it. Use a private message to send this info if you must.
- Don't accept a friend request from someone you don't know in person. It may be tempting, but remember that those pictures could be anyone!
- If you upload pictures through your phone or an Apple device, you can turn off the feature that tags your photo with the location where it was taken.
- If you list or post your favorite activities or clubs, limit the information so someone would not be able to locate you at a specific time and place.
- "Checking in" to a location with an app such as Foursquare or Facebook can alert any number of strangers to your

location (at the very least, it alerts people that you are not at home). It's usually safest to simply text those people you want to catch up with.

- Don't update online statuses so that a stranger could easily track where you are at all times.

The Internet can be a lot of fun, and what's available online grows and changes all the time. But if you're aware of the features, then no matter what the latest methods are, you can be wiser about how you use them.

Whether it's Facebook or another type of online community (or even a campus forum), be cautious about who has access to your information. Do not allow anyone with a computer connection access to things like your phone number, address, or whereabouts. Keeping up with privacy settings requires some online maintenance. Just like you need to take your car in for oil or to get your tires rotated, you'll want to check your account and privacy settings each month to be sure they are current and safe. Be sure to ask yourself these questions about your privacy settings:

- Who can access my profile, and what can a stranger see?
- Who has access to my photos or other information?
- Who can see where I am?
- What third-party applications have access to my information?
- What can someone find out about me from my profile?

Online Relationships

We'll talk more about relationships in a few chapters, but for now let's take a look at relationships with people you've met primarily online or through texting. If you have a relationship with someone who exists almost exclusively online (through IM, text, or e-mail), there may still be a gap between what you think you know about the person and what you really do know.

A lot can be hidden in online relationships, so you'll need to be careful to protect your heart—and yourself. Be sure you don't neglect in-person relationships in favor of the online ones. If you get together with the person (and here we're talking about someone you just don't know very well as opposed to someone you've never met at all), go to a public place and don't go alone. Always have someone else with you, at least at a table nearby.

Identity Theft

Identity theft is another reason to keep personal information offline. While all the privacy information we've already covered will help with avoiding identity theft, there are some additional tips you'll want to make note of:

- Change your passwords regularly, and don't use names or dates that people can easily discover.
- Don't put your date of birth online (or at least not the year).
- Don't ever give your password out to someone through e-mail or text.

- If you get a phone call or e-mail from someone claiming to represent a bank or credit card company, don't give any information out. Hang up and call the bank or credit card company directly using the information on the back of your card. The bank may need you to forward the fraudulent e-mail to them, so don't delete it until they say it's okay.

Room Safety

As you grow more comfortable on campus, it can be easy to get lax about locking your doors and keeping the things you treasure out of sight. Your room probably has quite a few valuables in it at any given time, from laptops to e-readers to cell phones and cameras. Even your textbooks can be valuable to someone looking to make a quick buck. Be sure to always carry your keys with you and lock everything up.

It's also a great idea to take inventory of everything you have in your room and keep it somewhere safe. If there is a break-in or theft, you'll want to be able to quickly figure out what's missing. Having that inventory will be extremely helpful. Also, you may want to invest in a safe or lockable storage container.

There are a number of great programs you can install on your phone or laptop that can thwart thieves. Software can be installed on your laptop that will not only help track it down but also remotely wipe your hard drive to protect your information from falling into the wrong hands. The professionals at electronic and computer stores should be able to make a recommendation for the best software for your items.

Along with this, be sure to back up all of your data from your phone and laptop to another source. You can use a hard drive, but because a hard drive can also be stolen, you might want to get a subscription that will back up your data to another location. Again, you can ask for advice from the professionals about the best service for backing up your data. The following are a few you can look into as you begin thinking about this: CrashPlan, Carbonite, and Mozy. They all do this for a yearly fee, but it's worth it to keep all of your data safe in case of a theft or even just a computer failure.

CrashPlan   Carbonite   Mozy

Be Safe, but Don't Fear

This has been a lot to ponder and we've talked about some pretty scary situations, but it's likely all stuff you've been aware of. Be smart about your choices, but don't live in fear. For some reassurance, read these amazing Scriptures: Isaiah 41:10; 2 Corinthians 10:4; 2 Peter 1:3; 1 John 4:4,18.

7

Clean Sweep

What would you consider yourself on a scale of 1 to 10, 1 being a total slob and 10 being a clean freak? Chances are you'll meet people on campus, in your hall, or even in your room with a number quite different than yours. In this chapter, we'll look at cleanliness and hygiene because when you're living in close quarters with a lot of people, it's just something that is going to come up.

Before you even go to school, you and your parents will have to fill out a lot of medical forms, you'll need a physical, and you may even need shots and vaccines. Your doctor will be able to help you and your parents decide what you need to get, but your school will have certain requirements as well. If your doctor recommends a vaccine (even if it's not required), you should seriously consider getting it. Be sure to make the visit to the doctor well in advance because not having all of your medical paperwork could delay your arrival on campus.

Clean Space

Living in a dorm with a roommate can be a fun experience, but every single person will have a different level of cleanliness. Some people care about how neat and clean things are, and others don't.

The following quiz might help you determine where you fall on the cleanliness scale. If you're game, share the questions with your roommate and see how he or she answers. You might be able to head off some future issues by talking ahead of time about things that bug you.

Rate yourself using this scale:

1 (never) 2 (rarely) 3 (sometimes)
4 (most of the time) 5 (all the time)

_____ 1. I like to keep my stuff clean and organized.

_____ 2. I do my laundry regularly.

_____ 3. I like to keep the bathroom clean.

_____ 4. When I clean, I do it thoroughly.

_____ 5. Dust bothers me.

_____ 6. I hate leaving dirty dishes around or in the sink.

_____ 7. I toss garbage right away and take out the trash frequently.

_____ 8. I need to have the room clean and clutter free to relax.

_____ 9. I worry about germs, bacteria, and mold.

_____ 10. I stick to a cleaning schedule so things don't fall behind.

If most of your answers are 4s and 5s, you're already pretty serious about cleanliness. However, since you could be living with someone who is the exact opposite, you'll want to find ways for both of you to be comfortable in your room. If your answers were mostly 1s, 2s, or 3s, you may need to strive to be more diligent about cleaning your room and bathroom so that you and your roommate can stay healthy. You also may end up with someone who wants everything clean at all times, and that may be an adjustment.

Cleaning Schedule

Cleaning supplies should be on your list of things to bring with you to school. It's a great idea to have all the supplies you need stored in a bucket or other container so they're easily accessible. Decide how often you want to be sure the bathroom gets cleaned thoroughly. Weekly is a good starting point. In between cleanings, you can use disinfectant wipes to wipe down surfaces quickly. Don't forget to do the doorknobs! Doorknobs are frequently forgotten and can harbor all sorts of germs.

You can stay on a regular cleaning schedule all year, but you'll want to do some extra cleaning and disinfecting if anyone becomes ill. Use a disinfectant to spray the room, and make sure that you wash your hands regularly with soap and water. It sounds silly, but it's actually the easiest way to avoid spreading illnesses when you're living in close quarters.

The surfaces in your room should be wiped down (including doorknobs, remote controls, closet handles, and so forth) and vacuumed regularly if you have a rug. If you don't have a rug, use a broom and mop to keep the floors clean. Sheets and bedding should be washed every two weeks unless someone's been sick. Anytime someone is ill, make sure you clean, wash, and disinfect. You'll also want to replace toothbrushes after being sick to avoid re-infecting yourself.

Remember, if you keep up with the cleaning schedule throughout the year, not only will it help you stay healthy but when it comes time to check out at the end of the year, you won't be breaking your back trying to get the soap scum off the shower walls or dirt out of the carpet.

How to Avoid Being the Clean Freak

When everyone first gets to school, most people are fine with talking about cleaning schedules and the fact that someone is going to have to clean the bathroom. But after the first couple of weeks, when the novelty of being away at school has worn off, you'll probably find that some people start "forgetting" to clean.

Instead of having to remind someone to clean as if you're the room mom or dad or complain constantly that you're the only one doing any cleaning, try to preempt the problems. Take the schedule you make up and print it out so that everyone's cleaning days are clearly assigned. Post it on the wall in your room (if it's in the bathroom, it may smudge from the moisture). Create a place on the schedule for signing off after completing each task. This keeps each person accountable. It doesn't mean you won't still have problems from time to time, but at least you've created an objective way to deal with it.

Your cleaning bucket should include:

- Sponges
- Disinfectant wipes (for quick wipe-downs in between scrubbing)
- Paper towels (to wipe down toilet and mirrors)
- Windex or comparable cleaner (for the mirrors)
- Multipurpose surface cleaner (409, Lysol, Clorox)
- Tile cleaner (be sure it contains disinfectant and soap scum remover)
- Toilet bowl cleaner with bleach (be sure you also purchase a toilet brush)
- Lysol (or other room disinfectant spray)
- Swiffer wipes (for easily dusting the room surfaces)
- Rubber gloves

Protecting Your Feet

Whether you share a bathroom with just a couple of other people or a whole hall, wearing flip-flops in the shower can keep your feet cleaner and healthier in communal living spaces. You'd be surprised at how many funguses and other bacteria can enter your system through a small cut on your foot. In addition, having a handy pair of flip-flops or other slip-on shoes is great for running down the hall. Going barefoot in hallways or in public bathrooms will expose you to more bacteria and illness.

FROM THE TRENCHES

Definitely bring shower shoes if you have a community bathroom. (Flip–flops will do.) Hall showers could be used by at least twenty different people, and there is no telling what could be on that floor! A shower caddy is also handy for keeping all of your shampoo and such together.

Cleanliness and Health

Cleanliness in your dorm room and bathroom is not simply a matter of style — it's a matter of health. You will be far more likely to pass germs and sickness back and forth if you aren't consistent about cleaning. Being ill at school makes it harder to study, harder to get to class, and harder to do your best. You can't completely avoid illness no matter what you do, but doing whatever you can to lower your risk of getting sick is a good thing.

If you approach the cleanliness subject from a health standpoint (rather than a personal-preference standpoint), it can help everyone get on the same page without feeling attacked.

When Sickness Strikes

Even if you've done everything you can to avoid getting sick, you will probably do so at some point during college. What do you do?

Before you leave for school, be sure you and your parents know exactly what your health insurance covers. College students can typically stay covered under their parents' policy, but there's a good chance you'll have to use the "out of network" provisions unless you're going to school very close by. If you are in another state, that may add an extra layer of uncertainty. But rather than waiting until you get sick, figuring it out beforehand will save time and stress.

Before you get to school:

- Review your insurance policy or call the insurance company to see what the rules are.
- Make sure you have your own insurance card or at least a copy of your parents' card so that all of the information is available.
- Find at least three places near the school that accept your insurance. Make sure at least one of the options is a 24/7 urgent care center. Write down the names, addresses, and phone numbers of all three options.
- Figure out how you would get there. Is there a car service you can call? Is there public transportation you can use? Can the school transport?
- You can record some of this information at the end of this book in the resource section.

Many minor illnesses can be handled with over-the-counter medications. You can take something to help with the effects of hay fever, allergies, and annoying colds. It's a great idea to have a small medical kit with you to keep everything all in one place. You will want to check with your university about medications and what their policies are concerning students having them in the dorms.

If you do have any special conditions such as asthma, severe allergies, diabetes, or epilepsy, you'll need to take time to train those around you about what they should do in an emergency. The more information you provide them, the easier it will be for them to respond quickly and confidently if there's a problem. And even if you don't have any special medical conditions, you may be the one who needs to act in an emergency, so take the time to really listen to the procedures.

Things to have in your medical kit:

- Any specialty medications (EpiPens, diabetes supplies, inhalers)
- Ibuprofen/acetaminophen pain relievers
- Decongestant/antihistamine
- Antibiotic ointment
- Anti-itch cream
- Bandages (in various sizes)
- Vitamins
- Anti-diarrheal/antacids/anti-nausea products
- Cough syrup/cough drops

Many of these items will be available at your campus bookstore to restock as needed, but it's a good idea to have them on hand when you arrive so you don't have to go out when you're feeling bad already. And it's usually cheaper to buy them at stores like Walmart or Target rather than the bookstore.

Most colds will get better on their own in seven to ten days. You may not feel great, but you should be able to function and go to class with the help of some over-the-counter medications. If you're throwing up, running a fever, or not getting better, your next stop should be your college health center.

Every campus has someone there to give you advice on what to do. The level of care you'll receive varies with the size of your school. Some large universities have the means to run tests for strep and flu, while others may check your temperature, give you a bag of salt to gargle with, and send you on your way.

It's no fun being sick, especially when you're away from home. Your university health center will send you to the hospital if you are severely ill or can help you get to a well-equipped clinic if necessary. Either way, unless you're admitted to the hospital, you may have to recover in your dorm room. Make sure you stay hydrated, try to eat (ask your roommate to bring back crackers or dry bread from the cafeteria), and hang in there.

Germ-Swapping Don'ts

Clearly, avoiding illness should be high on your list of priorities. The trouble is that people are often most contagious just before they get symptoms. So just because everyone seems healthy today doesn't mean they will be healthy tomorrow. Here are some ways to keep the germs away:

- Keep your toothbrush and toothpaste covered and don't share them. Because a toothbrush can touch the top of the toothpaste, it's an easy way to spread infection.

- Wash your hands effectively. Washing your hands is the easiest way to stay healthy. Use soap and warm water and wash for as long as it takes you to hum "Happy Birthday."
- Don't share utensils, cups, water bottles, straws, or lip balm. You don't know what someone else has, so don't expose yourself.
- Throw out spoiled food. You will likely have a small fridge in your room as well as snacks and other food. Go through your fridge every week or two and throw out spoiled food or expired milks and yogurts. Food poisoning is a nasty illness that you'll definitely want to avoid.
- Wipe down doorknobs. Yes, we keep saying this, but doorknobs are the most forgotten spot, and because everyone touches them, they need daily attention.

These may seem like things that aren't such a big deal, but because you can't know someone's medical history and someone may not even know he or she is sick, it's best for people to keep their germs to themselves. What if that friend has a cold sore in his mouth and gives it to you by sipping on your Coke? What if the girl next door uses your toothpaste and discovers the next day she's got the flu? Again, doing these things doesn't mean you'll never catch a nasty bug, but it reduces your risk, and that may be enough.

Hall Bathrooms

Depending on the dorm you are in, you may be sharing a bathroom with one other room or with your entire hall. If it's a hall bathroom, there are a few extra considerations for you. Even though the bathroom may be maintained by your college or university, it's hard to say whether that level of maintenance will be enough. So that's where it's still a good idea to have a cleaning kit, especially disinfectant wipes to give your space a quick wipe-down before you use it. You'll also want to always wear shower shoes or flip-flops even to just go in to brush your teeth.

By preparing yourself with cleaning supplies and a plan before going away to school, you'll be on the right track to staying healthy.

Healthy Relationships

Whether you have several friends going to the same college or you don't know a soul, you will have the chance to meet a lot of new people. For those who are a bit more introverted, meeting people might seem rather scary; outgoing people may be looking forward to the challenge. Even if you were socially comfortable in high school, you may find college slightly overwhelming at first. You've got to give yourself time to adjust to the new environment and realize that you will have different kinds of relationships. You may become great study partners with someone in your statistics class but not really hang out with him other than that. Your roommate may become your best friend or someone you just share a space with. Maybe you will end up hanging out with the guys in your hall, or maybe you'll hang out with people from the fourth floor instead.

Let's look at some of the ways to meet a wide range of people so that you're sure to find a few good friends.

School Orientation

Take advantage of any orientation activities your school offers. Make sure you spend time mingling and meeting others. You may not click with everyone, but finding even a few people who seem like good friend matches can give you a start. You don't have to go to every activity, but don't skip them all either. Find a few that sound like fun and go. You never know whom you might meet!

FROM THE TRENCHES

Leave your dorm room door open the first couple of weeks when you're doing homework or just hanging out. This way, people from your hall can feel free to stop by to introduce themselves. It's a great way to make new friends!

Sports

If you play sports, teams are a great way to meet people who already love something you love. School teams have more intensity to them than intramural sports do, but both can offer some friendship possibilities.

There's a Club for That!

What do you like to do? Gardening? Yoga? Running? Filmmaking? Performing? Student government? Journalism? Whatever your activity or interest, there is sure to be a club that will offer you the chance to meet others who like the same things as you. It's also easy to start your own club if there isn't already one in existence for your area of interest.

Because of all your other responsibilities at school — namely, going to class and studying — you'll probably want to start off slowly. Pick a couple of things you are most passionate about and try them first. You can always branch out and add activities when you're able.

FROM THE TRENCHES

You don't have to join every organization — or any, for that matter. Just make sure you have an interest in what you join and enough time for your schoolwork.

Serving Others

A number of student organizations exist to help serve people in a variety of ways. Serving side by side with others is a great way to meet people while at the same time genuinely contributing to your new community. You can also find ways to contribute to society, meet people, and learn things in your chosen field of study. Are you considering becoming a history major? Perhaps there's a preservation society on campus. Thinking about teaching special needs kids? There are programs in which college students volunteer and work with special needs students on the weekends, giving the parents a respite and you valuable experience. Maybe

Find an opportunity in your area at Volunteer Match.

you're a political science major and can volunteer during an election campaign. There are also places (such as homeless shelters and food banks) that can always use extra help.

Classes and Study Groups

Don't underestimate those sitting right next to you in class or how helpful a study group can be. During your first couple years in school, you'll frequently be taking general education requirements that allow students to be mixed up. But you may also begin taking classes in a major field that contains people who will be taking classes with you throughout your college career. Either way, getting to know those around you may yield valuable friendships.

Roommates

Your roommate will probably be the very first person you meet on campus. Some schools send you information about your roommate to help you get in touch with one another before you get to campus, so you might have already chatted with the person. But even if you've talked on the phone or exchanged messages, you don't really get to know someone until you meet him or her and live together in the same room. You don't have to become best friends, but you will have to find a way to get along.

Communication will be very important as you walk through your relationships with your roommate, suitemates, and hall mates. People cannot read your mind, and you can't read theirs, so it's best to make sure you communicate about your expectations and any issues you might be having. Even if you do become best buds with your roommate, at some point there will be conflict over something. It just comes with the territory when living with people in a highly stressful environment.

Fortunately, there are some things you can do to reduce conflict and find good resolutions to issues when they arise.

FROM THE TRENCHES

You don't have to be best friends with your roommate. Often roommates get along great, but not always. When you need to escape, have other close friends so you don't have to stay and stew in your room.

Communicating the "I LUV" Way

The first thing you should do is make sure you talk about the problem in a calm environment, and don't try to do it while rushing off to class or when you're overly upset. Schedule a time and place to talk calmly. Then just remember the acronym I LUV.[1] These guidelines are to be used throughout your conversation and aren't necessarily in any kind of sequence.

I is for "I" Language. Try to use the word *I* instead of the word *you*. Anytime you use *you*, it can feel as though you are attacking the other person. Instead, focus on communicating how you feel:

- Rather than "You always leave hair all over the bathroom and it's gross," try "I am really uncomfortable with how dirty the bathroom is."

- Rather than "Your music is always too loud," try "I really need to study for this exam tomorrow, and the music is making it hard for me to concentrate."

When you focus your language, you also focus the conflict on the problem at hand rather than making it a personal attack.

L is for "listening." When the other person is talking, give him or her your full attention and really listen. Think about making eye contact, and if you're unsure about what is being said, ask questions to make sure you've heard correctly. Listening *actively* is when you're trying to understand what the other person is saying and how he or she is feeling. It's important to share how you are feeling, but it's equally important to be attentive to the other person's side. You might be surprised by what you learn when you're willing to hear another viewpoint.

U is for "understanding." Understanding involves trying to listen and respond to what the other person is saying. It doesn't mean you have to agree with everything being said, but you should be able to state his or her perspective by saying, "I understand that you're feeling . . ." For example, "I understand that you're upset because I'm not letting you get to sleep when you want to." It's a way for you to prove you've heard the other person's perspective and clearly understand that viewpoint. If you don't understand something correctly, it gives the other person a chance to share it in a different way.

V is for "validation." This is similar to understanding, but it involves going one step further by acknowledging that the other person's perspective is valid. You value what the other person is saying—and him or her as a person—and it's through the validation that you will actually be able to make the change. If you value another person, it makes it easier to adjust and change something that is a problem. An example of this would be saying, "I understand that you're upset with me for not letting you get to sleep, and you're right—you should be able to go to bed when you need to." Just remember, validation doesn't end with a statement; you have to prove it with your actions.

These guidelines are useful for both when you're approaching someone with a problem or a person is approaching you. Does it mean that every conflict will get sorted out with a quick conversation? Unfortunately, no. Not everyone is reasonable to deal with. Not everyone is willing to see things from another's point of view. But it's a good starting point.

FROM THE TRENCHES

Always address roommate issues as soon as they come up. If you let something slide the first time, it will just continue to bother you until you can't take it anymore. Your roommate may not even be aware that what he or she is doing bothers you.

Adjustment and Flexibility

Living with other people requires us to be flexible and adjust to other people's needs and feelings. What you are comfortable with, your roommate may not be. Will you ignore your roommate's feelings, or will you make adjustments? Being willing to be flexible and understand someone else's needs and feelings will help you as you try to decide when to have a discussion about something that's bothering you.

We can control only our own choices and decisions, so there may be times you'll have to let something go even if it bugs you. But what do you do if it's something you just can't let go—something that is affecting your academics or is breaking regulations or laws?

When Communication Isn't Working

If you've gone to the person you're having trouble with and you're not getting anywhere, it may be time to go to the next level, and in a dorm situation, that would be your resident assistant (or RA). Essentially, what we've been talking about is the Matthew 18:15-17 process. First you go to the person directly, but if he or she doesn't listen, you bring in others to help.

Your RA has been prepared and trained to deal with conflicts, so don't feel as though you're bugging him or her. Your RA may even have some ideas for something else you can try before you have to do a sit-down all together. But in the event that the RA feels as if a sit-down is in order, go ahead and be honest, still using the communication guidelines we already talked about.

If more drastic measures are needed—such as changing rooms or bringing in higher authorities within the school—your resident assistant can help you walk through it. It may be hard to decide between living with the problem and moving rooms, but both are usually viable options. Your environment at school is stressful enough without adding in a problem living situation.

If it's impacting your academics, serious consideration should be given to making a change. Only you can really make that call, but wise counsel from your parents, trusted friends, and your resident assistant can help.

Sororities and Fraternities

Everything you join and become involved with has advantages and disadvantages. The big question will be, is a certain group right for you?

Sororities and fraternities come in all shapes and sizes. There are ones that are focused on academics, some that are focused on service, and, yes, some pretty much focused on partying. If you decide to consider pledging, you'll want to be thorough in your research.

During your freshman year, that research can be simply observation. What are the reputations of the different chapters? Anytime you choose to join a group of people, you are choosing to align yourself with them, so is their reputation one you would feel comfortable being a part of?

Being Ready to Join

You've already applied to college, so you know how important it is to be well-rounded. You should not only make sure your grades are excellent but also get involved with extracurricular activities and community service. When you submit for sorority or fraternity recruitment, you'll get a chance to list those things to show your interests as well as what makes you unique and different.

Online Research

You should be able to narrow down the sororities or fraternities you might be interested in and read about them online. Visit the national chapter website and learn about how it got started as well as the school chapter website. This will likely give you only a basic overview, but their philosophy and values will give you a good starting point.

You can also use sites such as College Confidential or Greek Chat to ask questions and read forum posts from others who may have experience or advice to offer. Be warned that these are open forums, so the language and tone will vary with each person who comments. You'll run across conflicting and varied advice, but you also may find some great nuggets of wisdom in there too.

Your College Greek Office

If there are sororities and fraternities on your campus, there will be an official office that regulates the Greek system. Go and visit the office or call to get information about the overall process. This will be great information for you as you make your decision.

The university's office staff will be a help to you throughout the process, so don't hesitate to ask questions or seek advice. They've helped hundreds of students before you, so they'll be your best and most reliable source of information.

Ask Around

There are rules governing those who are part of a fraternity or sorority, so how much someone can tell you may vary. As you meet people who have decided to join a fraternity or sorority, ask them some general questions. Find out why they joined and why they enjoy being a part of it. Typically, they can answer general questions about Greek life rather than specific questions about their particular sorority or fraternity. If you talk to enough people, you'll start to get a sense of the different chapters they are involved with. You'll also want to begin finding out about the pledging process, recruitment (rushing), and the different expectations of the chapters, including time and financial commitments that would be required.

Grades Matter

Your academics are extremely important, and all sororities and fraternities have minimum GPA requirements. Some of them are set by national chapters, but the school chapter may have an even higher requirement. Make sure you have a sufficiently high GPA to qualify for recruitment and that you're also able to maintain it should you get a bid to join a chapter.

Questions to Ask

Keep in mind that you won't want to drill someone to find these answers out; you'll just want to make sure that, over the course of your research, you discover the answers:

- What is your philanthropy and how do you support it?
- How much are the dues and how often are they paid? Are there events the dues don't cover?
- How many required events are there per semester (on average)?
- What are the other time commitments?

- What are the traditions of the chapter?
- What is it like for newer members? Is there any mentorship available for them?
- What kinds of events are important to the chapter?
- How do you balance academics and Greek life?

Choosing to be part of your school's Greek system is a big decision, so consult with people you trust as you sort through the pros and cons.

Dating

It's true that some people will meet their future spouse in college, but it's also likely you may meet and date a few others before you find the one you will end up marrying. For that reason, you want to keep a healthy dating perspective as you navigate your relationships.

Dating and Studying

Keep in mind that your first priority at school is to get a great education. No matter what you choose to do as far as jobs and careers go after school, your education will have value that extends far beyond that piece of paper.

Anything that interferes with getting that education should be avoided. If you are able to carry on a dating relationship and still stay focused on school and get solid grades, then for you dating may be just fine. But it's also okay to put off serious relationships and concentrate on building friendships during this time of your life.

So how can you tell if a relationship is good for you? Here are some questions to consider:

- Is my relationship with this person positive and encouraging?
- Does this person challenge me to do my best?
- Does this person distract me from things (academics, friendships, or God) that are important?
- Does this person want the best for me?
- Does this person drain me or fill me?
- Does this person share my values and morals?
- Is this person able to admit when being wrong?
- Is this person able to adjust when needed?
- Does this person treat others with honor and respect?

This is not an exhaustive list, of course, but it can help you ask questions that may not readily come to mind. Falling for someone can make us listen to our feelings, and feelings can be funny things. They can lead us down paths that may be unhealthy or even downright dangerous. Choose to be wise about the relationships you invest your time and energy in because, as Proverbs 4:23 tells us, our hearts determine the course of our lives.

Getting to Know You

Before jumping into any exclusive relationship, it's a great idea to get to know someone outside of the dating relationship. When newly dating, people are on their best behavior and you may not get a good sense of how the person truly is. College is a fabulous environment to get to know people in group situations before making any decisions about dating.

But if you do choose to date, make a commitment to keep yourself focused on what you are there to do: get a great education. Agree together that you'll be a positive influence on one another and encourage each other in everything you need to do at school.

Trusted Advisors

As you cultivate friendships in school, you'll want to have a few people you can count on to give you honest advice. Trusted advisors are people willing to tell you what you *need* to hear rather than what you *want* to hear. We all need people like that in our lives, but it's even more important during the college years, when you are making relationship decisions away from your family and friends back home. Of course, if you have a good relationship with your family, hopefully you will seek their counsel as well, but someone right there at school may have valuable insight.

Where can you find trusted advisors? Well, if you're involved with any campus ministries or small groups (we'll talk more about these later), they are a great place to start. But a trusted advisor is simply someone who has wisdom, is discerning, and will speak the truth. If you keep your eye out for them, you can find friends like this.

Teachers and Tutors and Assistants, Oh My!

Over the course of your college career, you'll encounter dozens of various professors, teaching assistants, and tutors. Some of them you will enjoy immensely and look forward to going to their classes and hearing their instruction; others you may dread. Some you will learn a lot from, and some you may not.

The kind of school you go to will determine a lot about the challenges you'll face with instructors. If you go to a small private school or Christian college, you'll have a completely different experience from going to a large state university. A liberal college will be different from a more conservative one. Hopefully you visited all of the places you considered attending and have chosen one where you'll fit in well. But even then, every professor will be as unique and varied as your classmates.

Choosing Your Professors

For the first semester, you may have simply been assigned classes based on your requests, but you can make changes to your schedule during a set time period after you arrive at school. Although the times and days classes are held will weigh heavily into which ones you take, you may find you can take the same class from several different professors. In that case, you may want to do a little research by asking upperclassmen about the professors. If not, you can look online at www.ratemyprofessors.com. After looking up your school, you'll find a list of professors with ratings and comments from those who have taken the class. Not only can you get a sense of how students liked the class overall but you can even get some tips on that professor's teaching style (like whether exams focus on the lectures or textbooks). Keep in mind that as with any review site, you'll get a wide range of opinions, but it can still be a very helpful resource when you don't know who to ask for teacher advice.

Getting Extra Help

At the beginning of the semester, you'll likely get information about all of your professors' office hours. If you're having trouble with something in class, go to your professor to get some clarity about whatever might be confusing you. Don't wait too long to get the help you need.

In general, the biggest difference between high school and college is there are fewer grades in college; therefore, each grade counts more. If you fail one quiz, it will bring down your overall grade more significantly than it might have in high school. If you don't understand the material or the assignments and stopping by the professor's office hasn't helped, check to see about getting a tutor.

Most schools have some sort of system in which you can find students or teaching assistants who offer extra help to students in various subject areas. There is usually a fee for this service, but it is cheaper to pay for the extra help than having to retake the class or repair the damage to your GPA. You may be able to find some free help by joining a study group (or creating one!) for that class. Make sure you invite people to join who are doing well in the class. And you never know when you might be able to return the favor. Someone from your hall might be great at science but need help with essays and you're the opposite. It's worth checking around.

Coworkers

College is pretty expensive, and many students hold down on-campus or off-campus jobs to help supplement their income during the school year. It helps to provide for such essentials as textbooks and school supplies, or it can just be for extra pocket money. Either way, having a boss and coworkers is another opportunity for improving your communication skills and developing relationships.

The communication tools we talked about earlier can be very helpful if there's a problem at work or with a coworker. You may find some great friends at work, or you may not click with them at all. Either way, you don't want your work situation to be miserable. When choosing a job, think through what would work best for you and not add extra stress. Are you someone who would thrive with the constant activity of food service, or would the quieter atmosphere of shelving books at the library fit you? Only you can tell, but the type of job you choose will likely give you coworkers with the same bent as you.

Don't let yourself get pressured into doing things you don't want to do. If your coworkers all want to go out after work and you need to go back to study (or just sleep), don't be afraid to say so. And the reverse is also true. If you invite others to join you and they have to turn you down because of a conflict, you should be understanding and give them a chance to come when it's a better time for them.

Shifting Family Relationships

You're an adult, and even though you still have parents back home, being away at school means you will be making your own decisions on a regular basis: what you eat, what you do, where you go, and whom you're with. For some, that change might be a pretty big leap; for others, you may have already been living that way at home. But for everyone, there is a shift in the family dynamics when you go off to school. It's a wonderful time of growth where you can try out your life navigational skills in an environment that is fairly safe. But while you may enjoy this newfound freedom, your family relationships shouldn't be neglected.

If you've never been particularly close with your parents, you'll probably need to make an effort to stay in touch and fill them in about what's going on. Set a time, say once a week, to call home and catch up with everyone. Making that effort honors them and is a respectful gesture worth making. (If you're the type who's not going to call your parents when you're in a tough situation, make sure you cultivate those trusted advisors we talked about earlier to help you when you're struggling.)

If you are close to your parents, college can be a transition in a different way. Even though you won't have them right there to talk with every day, they're just a quick text or phone call away. Your challenge will be weighing when to call and when to work through something on your own first. Think of problems as "major issues" and "minor issues." Major issues are things that affect your academics or your physical or mental health in such a way that they are interfering with your ability to live life. Minor issues are things that are an annoyance or a nuisance but aren't interfering in a major way.

You will likely have to handle a myriad of minor issues all the time at school, everything from dealing with a group project in your economics class to finding time to get to the grocery store. You made it into college and worked hard all through high school, so you'll be up to the challenge of handling most of the minor issues on your own.

But when major issues happen, getting your parents' feedback and advice can be invaluable. Hopefully, your parents will be able to give their opinions and then still allow you to make a decision and follow through. They've walked a few years ahead of you, so their perspective can be very helpful.

FROM THE TRENCHES

One of the biggest college myths is that you aren't being healthy and independent if you call home every other day. Sometimes you should troubleshoot things on your own, but also feel free to call Mom and Dad when you need to. You might call more frequently when the school year first starts, but this will likely balance out as you find your comfortable routine.

Getting Your Parents to Let Go

And some of you may have "helicopter parents," termed such because they hover nearby constantly. If yours are helicopter parents, you may need to set some boundaries yourself. For example, you can let them know you can talk to them only once a week so that you can concentrate on academics and developing relationships at school. It may take some insistence on your part, but a good balance between honoring them and still giving yourself the space you need is a good place to shoot for. You might even commit to a specific time to talk each week.

Visiting Home

If you are attending school far away, how often you go home may be affected more by flights and school breaks. But for those who live within driving distance, heading home on the weekends to see friends and others might be very appealing. But try not to, at least at first. Give yourself some time to get to know people at school. The easier pace of the weekend is a great time for catching up with schoolwork and building new friendships. All relationships take time to develop and grow, and you won't have that time if you skip out every weekend to go home and hang out with old friends.

Give yourself the first six weeks to stay at school, meet new people, and try new things. Most schools have a fall break in which you'll have a longer weekend to go home and visit. The relationships you have back home won't disappear, and if you explain to your friends and family about needing to create a new place for yourself at school, they can support you by not pressuring you to come home.

Long-Distance Relationships

It can be rather difficult for a girlfriend or boyfriend left behind to feel secure enough to let you go and immerse yourself in college. The best thing you can do is talk about what each of you needs from the other. Maybe you can set up once-a-week Skype visits so you can "see" each other face-to-face. Maybe you can plan some specific times to get together so that both of you know what to expect.

It's certainly not impossible to maintain this type of relationship, but you will both be growing and changing in ways you may not expect. Be prepared to do a lot of adjusting. The best way to keep issues from becoming bigger problems is to talk about them. Be honest about how you're feeling.

Church Family

You'll likely find that the churches in the surrounding area welcome college students to come and worship with them. Some might even provide transportation, and many have special programs that can link you to people who will offer support or friendship.

How do you go about finding a church? Well, Google can probably give you a good starting point for finding out about the different denominations in your surrounding area. Church websites usually give insight as to what types of college programs are provided. At that point, you can simply call and ask about visiting. Your college student life office may also be able to provide a list of churches in the area that offer transportation to students.

This becomes a second really good reason to stay at school those first few months: You can pick a church and visit. Keep visiting churches until you find a place that feels right to you — a place that bases its beliefs and philosophies on the Bible and where you feel as though you will be able to grow closer to the Lord. Invite a friend or two to join you as you look for a church home away from home. Visit your friends' churches as well. You may learn quite a bit by seeing the different styles of worship and how they share the Bible in different church families.

On-Campus Ministries

If you go to a Christian school, it is likely your campus will have a robust spiritual program and a variety of events and activities to get involved in. Find out how your school communicates these opportunities. You should try to find ways to reach outside your comfort zone and try new things. Maybe small prayer groups aren't "your thing," but if you give them a chance, you might find one to be a tremendous blessing. It's like food: You really can't say whether you like something unless you've given it a try.

Even if you don't go to a Christian school, there are amazing organizations to be a part of that can help you plug in with other people who share your beliefs and values. Every campus has active religious organizations, and you can usually find a list of them on the student life section of your school's website. You actually may be overwhelmed by all the choices! Some of the campus ministries may be run by local churches or regional groups, but there are also a number of national and international ministries that maintain chapters on campuses around the nation. We'll take a closer look at these organizations in chapter 11.

The Navigators

Cru

InterVarsity   FCA

Getting involved in campus ministries can be an important part of developing positive relationships on campus. Campus ministries may be where you find those trusted advisors and friends who really understand what's important to you and will challenge you to be all God meant for you to be.

FROM THE TRENCHES

Get to know the upperclassmen. Just a few years ago, they were where you are. Learn from their mistakes; don't repeat them.

Building new relationships takes an investment of time and energy on our parts, but they are worth it. If you commit yourself to trying new things, you'll also discover new friendships that could last a lifetime.

Struggling with Change

While college can be full of exciting opportunities, the drastic change in life circumstances can be difficult. Not everyone thrives on change. Not everyone loves new adventures. You may be one of those people looking at college with a bit of trepidation, wondering if you'll make friends, wondering if you'll be happy there.

Don't worry; that's completely normal! But if that's how you're feeling, you'll want to take some steps that will help you make the transition. It may still be a challenge, but it's a challenge you can overcome.

The first thing to do is check your attitude. If you go into college expecting to hate it, expecting not to make friends, expecting to have problems, you will probably experience these things and more. This is more than a simple Pollyanna—be positive!—suggestion. If we think we won't enjoy something, we can't be in a position to enjoy it. Try to reframe your thinking and give yourself a small, attainable goal that will help you combat any tendency you have to give in to those negative feelings. Instead of "I'm not going to have anyone to talk to," decide "I'm going to try to meet at least one new person a day." Instead of "I'm not going to have anything fun to do," decide "I'm going to choose two activities or clubs to go to within the first month of school."

It can make a difference in how you approach school if you are proactive rather than negative.

Preparing Yourself

The next thing to know is that you'll have to give yourself time to adjust. Don't worry about people around you who may jump into school and within the first twenty-four hours seem to know everyone on campus and look like they've been there for four years instead of just two days. You can't compare yourself to how others jump in. They aren't you. You'll have to find the path that fits you and is right for the way God made you.

But it may take some time. The first couple of months, you have a lot of changes all at once, so you can't look at the first six weeks of school and assume that's what it will be like forever. It won't. Give yourself the entire first semester, even the first year, to adjust. That will give you time to continue trying new groups and activities if the first few you try aren't good fits.

College will be a brand-new experience, and no matter what you did or who you were in high school, you'll get the chance to really start focusing on who you are becoming—and that may be a different kind of person than you expected. Maybe you were a high school football or soccer star but aren't playing for your college team. That doesn't diminish your new role in college at all. Instead, it gives you the opportunity to figure out what will be important to you during college. Maybe high school was tough and you weren't that popular. Don't assume that will follow you. You may be surprised by those who are willing to offer friendship. Maybe you're one of the lucky few who know exactly what they want to do and you have the next four years mapped out. That's great, but don't forget to try new things. Sometimes students come into college expecting to go one direction and a fantastic class or teacher opens their eyes to new possibilities.

We can encourage you to expect that change and embrace it all day long, but if you had a fantastic high school experience, you might struggle with the idea of having to start all over and build new relationships. In reality, if you were popular and had lots of friends in high school, you should be well equipped to forge new friendships. But you can still end up feeling like a small fish in a much bigger pond.

Maybe you were valedictorian of your high school and the top kid in everything. In college, you may find multiple people who achieved the same honors sitting all around you. You'll suddenly find yourself surrounded by people with a similar drive and motivation as you. Resist the urge to get competitive. Work to do your best and really learn and your grades will usually reflect that. Make your college years count in the best possible way. If you expect change, it won't be so surprising and you'll be better able to adjust to your environment.

Family Changes

Another change you should expect is that it may be different going home. When you left home, you were still in that high school phase of life, but when you go home for break, you'll have entered a new phase of young adulthood. You will be taking on lots of your own decision making, and there is no one at school you have to ask permission from if you want to stay out late or join an activity. The level of the change will vary depending on how much freedom you had before you left for school. If you had a lot of freedom already, you may find going home for breaks to be pretty similar to what you were used to.

But if you didn't have a ton of freedom, going home could be a rude awakening. Most conflicts at home occur because both sides have different expectations. You may expect that you will be able to come home to the same freedoms you've grown accustomed to at college, while your parents may expect you to return to the same rules and expectations you had as a high school student.

If you recognize that there may be differing expectations, you can avoid some potential conflicts by discussing them with each other and coming to an agreement. Creating a family contract can be a great way to make sure everyone is heard and can agree to the expectations.

Creating a Family Contract

So how do you go about creating a family contract? Well, a contract can be adjusted to fit any kind of family situation.

Step 1: Determine your expectations. In this first phase, each family member writes what his or her expectations will be regarding these topics:

- Curfews
- Asking permission to go places
- Mealtimes
- Assistance around the house/chores/responsibilities
- Household expectations for behavior (language, respect, fighting)
- Sibling dynamics
- Driving privileges
- Amount of time spent with family versus friends
- Any other specific area that is important to someone

Until you have been away at school for a few weeks, you probably won't have a good sense of what your expectations will be, so the best time to work on this is just before you come home. Talk to your parents about it and ask them to do the same thing.

Step 2: Set a meeting time. Next, family members will bring their expectations and sit down to discuss the similarities and differences of the lists. Start with places where there is agreement, and then move on to discuss where there are different expectations. For example, maybe you are expecting to spend lots of time with friends, and your family is expecting you to spend lots of time with them. Both sides should try to be flexible as you come to an agreement that meets the differing needs. This will probably be the hardest part of the process, but working through the differences like this will be far more productive than getting in a big fight over something later.

Step 3: Put it in writing. Once you've come to an agreement, write up what everyone has agreed to and have everyone sign it. This might seem like a pointless step, but having the actual documentation will help keep everyone on the same page.

Step 4: Make amendments. Don't assume that once you put expectations in writing that things won't need to change. You or your family may realize that something just isn't working and there is a need to revisit a certain issue. Allow everyone the ability to declare the need to take another look at the contract, discuss it, and make the necessary changes. The family contract should be flexible enough for the changing needs of you and your family.

Homesickness

Even if you don't expect to ever feel this (being one of those adventurous types), you might still find yourself feeling homesick from time to time. "Homesick" is a bit of a misnomer because it's not always about wanting to be back at your house; it's really more about longing for the way things used to be rather than simply being at home. It can also be a longing to feel the same way you might have at home, maybe safe and secure or even that you felt loved and understood better by people back home. All of those things can play into that overall feeling that is called homesickness. Again, it's perfectly normal.

For nagging feelings of homesickness, a simple call to your family can ease things. Maybe a visit from someone back home can help. Touch base with those you love, but continue to actively try new things and reach out to people around you at school. The more involved you get at school, the more you will begin to feel at home there, too. What you don't want to do is spend all your time wishing you were back home instead of trying to engage in the new opportunities around you.

FROM THE TRENCHES

Everyone experiences homesickness, but that doesn't mean you have to suffer through it alone. Find ways to connect with friends at school when you're missing home. Knock on your neighbor's door and see if anyone wants some company. Chances are the person might be feeling lonely as well.

Staying In Touch

You can stay in touch with friends and family back home very easily nowadays, and you should. Like most things in life, finding balance is the key. Enjoy your friends and family. Share all your new experiences and listen to what is going on with them. But definitely don't spend all your time communicating with those back home and none communicating with those at school with you. Make an effort in both areas and you'll find your world expanding in good ways.

Loneliness

This is pretty similar to homesickness, and, like homesickness, it's a bit of a misnomer. There you are, surrounded by thousands of new people on campus—how can you feel lonely? Well, you can, especially if you find yourself struggling to connect with those you meet early on. Maybe your roommate is already buddies with his soccer team and isn't all that interested in hanging out with you. And maybe those in the hall have connected with their room-mates and don't really notice that you don't have anyone to go to dinner with. You can find yourself feeling lonely. But like most things, your attitude toward loneliness is important in how you deal with it. Going to dinner by yourself now and then doesn't need to be the end of the world. We reflect and observe differently when we are on our own. Take it as a bit of a breather. But you also have a couple of other options.

Invite someone else. Meals are a great excuse to introduce yourself to someone and reach out in friendship. You could also ask to sit with someone once you get to the meal. You'll find that college is different from high school and, for the most part, many are will-ing to open doors of friendship. Feeling a bit lonely now and then is normal, but if you're willing to step out a bit and be the one to do the inviting, you may find that loneliness start to disappear.

 FROM THE TRENCHES

Download Skype. It is the next best thing to seeing your family and friends in person.

Skype

Depression

But what if what you're feeling—loneliness, homesickness, sadness—becomes more overwhelming than you can handle? What if your feelings are past that "nagging feeling" and you find yourself struggling to hold it together emotionally, crying yourself to sleep every night, or wanting to bail out and just go home? Everyone gets down now and then. You may feel grumpy, frustrated, or sad for all sorts of reasons. Maybe you didn't get enough sleep. But maybe your homesickness has reached the point of feeling depressed. Before we go too much further, let's look at a few symptoms of depression:

- Feelings of hopelessness
- Feeling helpless
- No motivation

We all have feelings of sadness, helplessness, or hopelessness at different times, so how do you know when what you're feeling is something more than that? You need to seek help if your feelings of depression really start to interfere with or negatively affect your daily life, such as in the following ways:

- Not wanting to go to class
- Not bothering to do assigned work
- Not wanting to eat
- Sleeping too much (not wanting to get out of bed)
- Insomnia (inability to sleep much at all)

- Not bothering to shower or take care of yourself in some way
- Not feeling pleasure in doing activities that once were pleasurable
- Feeling suicidal or having thoughts of wanting to end it all

If any of these things describes the level of your (or someone else's) depression, help is necessary. See page 127 for the "When You Need More Help" section later on in this chapter.

Stress and Anxiety

If there is one thing that every college student probably has in common, it's stress. You are going to feel stress from time to time. Everyone does. But how you deal and cope with stress is going to be very important as you head into college. First, let's take a little stress inventory to see what your stress level has been.

After reading the following statement, mark the answer that most describes you.

When I'm in school, on average I feel stress:

___ never

___ sometimes

___ frequently

___ all the time

As we mentioned, it's normal to feel stress now and then, but if you feel it "frequently" or "all the time," then you'll want to have a plan in place to cope with the new stressors of college.

Again, mark the answer that most describes you.
When I'm feeling stressed, I:
___ don't sleep
___ struggle to sleep
___ sleep, but maybe not as well as I normally do
___ sleep well

We already talked about the importance of sleep and how sleep can affect everything from academics to social situations to your overall health. Stress can impact your sleep in negative ways, so if you're already seeing a pattern of it hurting your sleep, you'll want to come up with some proactive ways to handle it. Don't worry — we'll give you some ideas!

What relaxes you? Are you able to settle down and enjoy a conversation or meal? What helps you de-stress? If you can come up with two things that help you, you're off to a great start. If you're struggling to come up with anything that helps you relax, you'll want to actively look for some things to help detox from the stress of college.

Two things that help me relax are _____
and _____.

Negative Coping Habits

Unfortunately, many people get in the habit of handling their stress in negative ways. As we mentioned, everyone feels stress now and then, but if you deal with your stress by doing such things as getting drunk, smoking cigarettes, or overeating, you run the risk of causing additional health problems. Here are some negative coping habits you'll want to avoid:

- Drinking/partying
- Smoking
- Caffeine dependence
- Other habitual drug use to stay awake/fall asleep
- Avoidance
- Lashing out/irritability/anger

Not only can these habits harm you or your relationships with others but they are not effective stress-management tools. So what can you do when you're feeling stressed?

De-Stressing Your Life in Positive Ways

It's critical to have a plan for managing your stress, so we'd like to encourage you to create a stress tool kit—things you can try at school to help you relax. This tool kit can be a great resource, and it will give you quick and ready options when you need them. Maybe you've already got some ideas on what relaxes you. That's great! But the more positive stress-management strategies you have in your tool kit, the better. Here are some ideas.

Exercise. Exercise has been proven over and over to help reduce stress, and it doesn't have to be lifting weights and running laps for an hour at a time. If you close your books and take a brisk walk, take a swim in the pool, or join a pick-up game of soccer, you'll naturally relax your body and mind. Keep an eye on your time and don't take up the whole afternoon, but by allowing yourself the chance to exercise, you'll return to your studies more refreshed and hopefully ready to work.

Have a quiet time. In this over-connected world, most of us just don't get enough quiet time. We all need quiet to clear our heads and settle our hearts. If you follow Christ, this is the time when you get quiet and connect with Him. This might mean reading the Word to see what God has to say to you, but overall this is the time to talk with Him and listen for what He might want to tell you. This quiet time can reenergize you in a number of ways. It can offer you great perspective and remind you to value the blessing of your education.

Read. Now, chances are that the idea of reading may be exactly what's stressing you out. If so, skip this one! But if you're someone who loves to read, reading something for fun may be just the thing to relax you a little before diving into studying for that big exam.

Journal. Sometimes we experience stress because we simply have too much going on inside our heads. Keeping a journal can be a great way to decompress and figure out whether it's that test stressing you out or if it's really your roommate. There are stressors we can't do anything about, and projects, exams, and papers are simply a part of college. But journaling can uncover some of the other things we may be fretting over. Once you uncover them, you will be better able to see if they are things you need to let go of (things you really can't do anything about) or things you need to deal with (maybe you need to drop out of an activity because you've taken on too much).

Listen to music. Something about listening to music can be completely relaxing. You can pop in your earbuds and take a walk or go find a quiet bench and people-watch while you settle down.

Play a game. Having fun playing a game can be exactly the kind of fun you need. Laughing and enjoying others can help you relax, and there are probably a few others around your dorm who could use the same kind of relief.

Volunteer at an animal shelter. Helping with animals can be a kind thing to do and can help relieve stress. If you love animals, being around them can be very enjoyable, and because students typically can't have pets on campus, it may be one of the few ways you can be around animals.

Get creative. Art can engage a whole different side of the brain, giving the other side a bit of a break. Even if you're not an artist, drawing, coloring, or painting can be relaxing and therapeutic. When's the last time you colored? You might be surprised at how much fun it is. You can also create an online photo album, put together a video, or go take pictures on campus.

Call a friend. Maybe you relax by being around or talking to people you care about. If so, you can call up a friend just to chat or invite him or her to do something enjoyable. Get off campus for dinner, for a hike, or to see a new movie.

Get outdoors. Being cooped up indoors can be very stressful for some people, so if that's you, get outdoors as often as you can. You can take a blanket and study in the sun. You may even find yourself more productive with your tasks if you do them in an enjoyable environment.

Join a club. Perhaps the things you love to do are not very convenient. Maybe you love rock climbing or skiing or horseback riding. It's worth a look to see if there's a club on campus that may go as a group to do those activities. You may not do them often, but having an activity to look forward to might be motivating.

Focus on today. In the book of Matthew, Jesus shared with His disciples about where their focus should be: "Give your entire attention to what God is doing right now, and don't get worked up about what may or may not happen tomorrow. God will help you deal with whatever hard things come up when the time comes" (Matthew 6:34).

Isn't that an amazing promise? It doesn't do us any good to get upset about what's coming, so when you're feeling stressed, make a list of what you need to do today and just focus on that. Figure out what you can reasonably accomplish in the time you have available, and only concern yourself with those tasks. Stressing over every paper and exam won't be productive, and you can deal with only what's right in front of you anyway.

These are just ideas to get you going in the right direction because you'll really need to find what works for you to relieve stress. Everyone is unique, so something that helps your roommate relax might not be the same thing that helps you relax.

Making a Stress Tool Kit

Write down at least five things that you think may help you relax when you're feeling panicked. You can start with things you already use to deal with stress and add in some other options. Maybe something we mentioned sounded like a good fit for you.

When I feel stressed, I'm going to try the following activities:

_____

_____

_____

_____

_____

When Stress Becomes Anxiety

Yes, everyone feels stress from time to time. Having your stress tool kit will help. But sometimes your stress level can get out of control, and you may need some extra help in learning to manage it.

Stress, if left unchecked, can start to overwhelm your life if you're not careful. It can also lead to using negative strategies just to get some relief. But that is not how you were meant to live. How can you tell if your stress has become an anxiety problem that you need to seek help for?

The general rule of thumb is that anytime you are experiencing things that interfere with your ability to function, you need to seek help. What might that look like?

- Excessive worry
- Anticipating disaster
- Not being able to relax
- Fatigue, headaches, stomachaches, nausea, trembling
- Trouble falling asleep or staying asleep
- Difficulty concentrating
- Avoiding life (classes, social situations, friends)

Typically, if these types of symptoms are occurring for months or are gradually getting worse, you might need help managing your anxiety. Anxiety disorders can develop and grow worse over time, so getting some support and advice is necessary.

When You Need More Help

At every school, if you're struggling to the point where you are not functioning very well academically, physically, or emotionally, then the best thing you can do for yourself is to reach out for help. Taking that first step to seek the help will be the hardest, but no one can do it for you. Even those around you who may be keenly aware that you're struggling cannot force you to seek help. You have to make that choice.

Every school has some sort of on-campus counseling center. If how you're feeling is interfering with your life, take the step and make an appointment. The people there have seen it all, and they'll know how to help. Don't be embarrassed. Don't be ashamed. Make the choice to seek help so that you can get better. All you have to do is make that initial appointment. When you make a counseling appointment, in most cases you'll be seen by someone for a screening.

What Is a Screening?

A screening is when someone sits down and talks with you about whatever you need to talk about. You can share how you're feeling, something that's happened, whatever the problems are. The person will likely ask lots of questions to get an understanding of your problem and then make recommendations on what to do next. Some ideas would be a tutor for a class you're struggling with, a group counseling session on campus with other students struggling with the very same issue as you, or individual counseling if there are multiple issues for you to sort through.

No matter the recommendation, the person at the counseling center can help you access those services. There is no shame in getting some help. You'd be surprised to learn how effective sitting down with a trained professional can be in helping you navigate your new world. Follow through with the recommendations — give it a try. It won't make things worse, and it could actually make things better!

A note about counseling: If you're a Christian at a secular college and would like to be referred to a Christian counselor, enlist your parents to help you find one nearby. You can conduct an online search or try a database service. Because you are likely under your parents' medical insurance, you should involve them in your decision to get some help. You don't have to explain every detail to them if you're not comfortable doing so, but they can help you access services outside the scope of your campus.

What If It's Not You?

Being in such close proximity with so many others, you often end up with a front-row seat to others' serious issues. What should you do? It's sometimes easy to just ignore the problems others are facing, but your roommate, your friend, or someone down the hall may really need your help. Dealing with those who are suffering can be exhausting at times, and it also may be tempting to just tell them to snap out of it or get over it, but he or she may not be capable of doing that. The person likely needs support and a listening ear but also may need a great deal more. How do you know the difference between when it's time to be supportive and when you might need to step up and intervene?

We've already covered depression and anxiety, two of the issues you're likely to see most frequently, but let's look at some other serious issues that, while less frequent, you will possibly see on campus. You can find more detailed symptoms of a variety of mental health issues on a reputable site such as the National Institute of Mental Health (www.nimh.nih.gov). Keep in mind that all you're looking for are general symptoms that may indicate a problem. It's not your job to diagnose. If you sense there is a problem, there probably is. The best thing you can do is speak up and try to get the person help. We'll talk more about that shortly. Here are some other issues you or someone close to you may experience.

Anorexia and Bulimia

There is a lot of information out there about this illness, so we'll go over just the basics here. The first thing you need to know is that it really is a serious illness and can be life-threatening. People who suffer with anorexia or bulimia need intervention to get well. They likely aren't capable of following through when they say, "I'll just start eating" or "I'll just stop throwing up." Also, someone who suffers with this may have been able to keep it a secret far better at home than in a dorm full of people, so this may be the first time someone recognizes the problem.

Signs of Anorexia
- Unhealthy and extremely low weight
- Very thin, yet talks about themselves as fat
- Does not eat or eats in very small quantities (overly concerned about portion size)
- Use of laxatives, vomiting, or extreme exercise to lose weight
- Lack of menstruation

Signs of Bulimia
- May be of normal weight but is still intensely unhappy with their shape or size
- Obsessed about body weight and food
- Eats large quantities of food and then purges (throws it up)
- Visits bathroom after every meal (hides bathroom visits)
- Uses fasting, laxatives, or excessive exercise to compensate for binge eating
- May have a chronic sore throat or bad breath from the purging

- Guys might be obsessive over "bulking up" or their muscle mass
- Guys often exhibit a warped sense of what their bodies look like and intense unhappiness with them

Excessive Exercise

Both bulimia and anorexia can have an "excessive exercise" component, but excessive exercise can impact those who do not have an eating disorder as well. Figuring out whether exercise is at healthy or unhealthy levels can be a bit tricky. Here are some questions that may help determine if there might be a problem:

- Is the exercise a priority over everything else (including classes)?
- Are you keeping up with all of your classes?
- Are you enjoying healthy relationships with others?
- Do you find that your need for exercise is greater than just about anything else?
- Is the duration of exercise excessive (hours and hours rather than thirty to sixty minutes per day)?
- Are you eating healthy, appropriate portions to compensate for the exercise?

If the exercise is keeping you from functioning in your academic or social life, there is likely a problem.

Self-Mutilation/Cutting

The official term for this is NSSI (non-suicidal self-injury), but it's frequently described as "cutting." People who engage in this behavior will deliberately cut themselves and usually hide it from others. The most obvious sign of this is cut marks on the person's skin. When asked about the marks, the person will frequently lie about the injuries. Other things you might see:

- Wearing long sleeves or pants even if the weather is warm
- Excessive concern about dressing in complete privacy
- Isolation from others
- Secretive activities or "hiding" behaviors
- Defensiveness or anger if asked about behavior

The National Institute of Mental Health indicates that one out of every ten college students engages in more than one hundred episodes of cutting behavior in his or her lifetime.[1]

Those who are injuring themselves need intervention, as this behavior is unlikely to just go away on its own. At the same time, pointing it out or trying to help is likely to result in some anger or defensiveness. Don't let that stop you from trying; just be prepared for it.

When It's Time to Intervene

If your friend is threatening to harm himself or others or if his life is "going down the tubes" (failing school, isolating himself, not functioning in some way), intervention is needed. Unfortunately, you can never make people receive help and it can be uncomfortable to say to someone, "You need help," but it's the most loving thing you can do for the person.

If it's an emergency and someone is making clear threats to kill himself or hurt someone else, you need to call 911 or the campus police department. If the suicidal thoughts are more "expressing a desire to die" rather than clear threats, a suicide hotline (1-800-SUICIDE) might be the best place to start. The people who answer those phones are well trained and will be able to help.

For someone who clearly needs help but perhaps it's not a life-threatening emergency, you can still intervene and assist in several ways:

- Encourage the person to make an appointment with the campus counseling department for a screening. Sit close by as he or she calls and sets it up.
- Go with your friend to the appointment. Taking that step is so hard; having someone to go with makes him or her far more likely to keep the appointment.
- Encourage the person to follow through with the recommendations. Offer to help with accountability. For example, if the counseling center recommends a group, find out when those meetings are and help your friend get to them.
- Remember that you're not responsible for your friend's choice to get help or not get help. All you can do is try. If

you've tried the above-mentioned suggestions and your friend is still resistant and fighting you, make sure you don't take on a burden you were never meant to carry. Pray for him or her, continue to be supportive and encouraging, but realize that the person has to make the decision to get healthy.

10

A Healthy Mind

You've gone to school to get an education and prepare for the life ahead of you. What a great opportunity! Sometimes we forget that those who are able to go away to college to completely focus on their education are in the minority of their peers. Many others have to work full-time and take classes here and there to complete their education. Many are never given the opportunity to go at all. When we really take a look at how blessed we are, it can help us value the privileges we've been given by God.

When we don't value what we've been given, we can end up squandering those blessings. You will be surrounded by all types of people with all types of values. Will you be like those who value their opportunities or those who squander them? Paul reminded the Romans that when they focused on God, they could keep from being negatively impacted by the culture around them.

Here's what I want you to do, God helping you: Take your everyday, ordinary life — your sleeping, eating, going-to-work, and walking-around life — and place it before God as an offering. Embracing what God does for you is the best thing you can do for him. Don't become so well-adjusted to your culture that you fit into it without even thinking. Instead, fix your attention on God. You'll be changed from the inside out. Readily recognize what he wants from you, and quickly respond to it. Unlike the culture around you, always dragging you down to its level of immaturity, God brings the best out of you, develops well-formed maturity in you. (Romans 12:1-2)

Regardless of whether you go to a Christian college or a secular one, you will have positive and negative influences all around you. In this chapter, we'll look at how to make the most of the tremendous opportunity you've been given and find ways God can help you develop that "well-formed maturity."

The Value of College

Let's face it: Your college degree will be valuable to you no matter what kind of career you go into. We don't know what our tomorrows will bring, and the career you think you want when you start college may not be where you end up when you graduate. That's okay. Some people know exactly what they want to do, while others waver, unsure of where their gifts and talents lie.

But college isn't just about certain courses or career paths; it's about growing and maturing as a person of wisdom. College is a great place to learn how to get along socially in an environment with a huge mix of people and values. You'll be learning how to challenge your mind with new concepts and tasks and making decisions on how to care for your physical body. And all of this happens in an environment where you can also pursue the gifts and callings God has already placed inside of you.

College has a lot going for it! But not everyone is going to receive the wisdom that's available to them. That's their choice. But will you? Will you pursue wisdom? You don't have to be passionate about every single class, as you'll probably have classes that are hard or boring. But even in those classes, you can learn something valuable if you choose to.

Organizing Your Academic Life

Even if you're not naturally an organized person, you're going to want to bring some organization into your life so that you can handle your course load. Here are some easy ways to help you stay on top of things.

Lay It All Out

Grab a good calendar with plenty of space. It can be one on your computer or a physical one. Make sure it's big enough that you're able to look at each month and get a sense of what's coming; your phone is too small to quickly show you what you need. Pick a different color pen or highlighter for each of your classes. Then review your syllabus (outline) from each class and write in every quiz, test, assignment, and paper on your calendar.

For larger assignments such as research papers, figure out the halfway point so that you have a clear date of when you need to be finished with 50 percent of the paper. Make sure that date is marked on your calendar as well.

TIP FROM THE TRENCHES

Get in the habit of writing down important information. Purchase a day planner to compile all the due dates for your papers and make a note on your phone to remind you what hours the cafeteria and library are open. If you schedule ahead for your homework time and downtime, you shouldn't be stuck pulling all-nighters every week.

Figuring Out What Classes You Need to Take

Many colleges and universities have required classes that you'll need to take in order to graduate. Try to take classes that will do "double-duty," meaning they will satisfy a major requirement as well as a general education requirement. Spend some time poring over those requirements as well as the requirements within your possible major so that you really know what you'll need to take and when. Talking to your advisor is also a great way to make sure you don't miss something important.

Map out possible course schedules for each semester over the next four years using those requirements (see pages 195–196). You'll have to make adjustments if you can't get into a certain class, and you may not know exactly what you'll take for a certain requirement, but you should have a couple of options ready to go. If you're not sure of your major, that's okay, but hopefully you have some idea so that you can take some of the early required courses to give them a try.

You may have come into college with AP (advanced placement) or IB (international baccalaureate) class credits and you've already satisfied certain requirements, so be sure you know what's covered and what's not. You probably have a faculty advisor to get advice from if you get stuck or are unsure about a requirement.

FROM THE TRENCHES

Do not procrastinate! It never helps, and you'll end up at the end of the semester with a ton of work and no time to do it. If you think, *Oh, I'll just do it later*, realize that the semester gets busier as you go along. When midterms and finals come around, you won't have that extra time you could have been working on papers, projects, and homework.

"I Don't Know What I Want to Do!"

That's okay! You may not be sure of your major, but you should know the types of classes that interest you the most. What were your favorite classes in high school? If you loved your science classes, explore the science or engineering majors. If you preferred English, look into English, communication, literature, and linguistics. If history was your thing, try a class in sociology, history, or international or cultural studies. Starting with your natural bent should get you going in the right direction. Your freshman year is a great time to try out classes you've never had the opportunity to take and see if something sparks your interest.

If you're really lost, though, you should visit the career planning department at your school. Most of them have assessments you can take to help you figure out what kinds of careers would suit you best. (It's basically a questionnaire that helps you look at your strengths, weaknesses, and interests and narrow down your career search.)

Books, Notebooks, and Folders
It seems like such an obvious thing, but having the necessary materials for every class is as important as showing up for those classes! You'll get a syllabus (or you'll be directed to an online syllabus) with all the recommended materials you'll need for the class. Make sure you have all those materials plus a way to keep them organized. Accordion folders with a secure flap can be very useful because they are usually big enough to slide a notebook into. Even if you plan to take notes on a laptop, you might still need a place to store any handouts that come your way.

Computer Backup
Be sure to designate a regular time (weekly is a great idea) to back up the information on your laptop. You might also want to back up your files if you're working on a particularly important paper or project. Having everything on an external hard drive can save your bacon if your computer fails, gets damaged, or gets stolen. It's also a good idea to have a backup stored off-site by purchasing a backup plan with such companies as CrashPlan, Mozy, or Carbonite. It's relatively cheap when you consider that all of your files will be safe somewhere else if the worst-case scenario happens.

Learning Styles

How do you learn best? Each professor is different in the way they test students. Some lecture and test primarily off your lecture notes, others expect you to know the book, and others test you on all of it. Ask around for tips on the best way to study for various professors and classes. You'll want to learn how to take solid notes. For some, note-taking can help solidify the ideas and help with retaining the new information.

If you're an "auditory learner"—meaning you like to hear the new information—then recording lectures may be a great idea. However, to make this a useful strategy, you really need to go back and listen to the lectures again in order to properly study. If you do listen to the lectures again, pull out the main ideas and write them down so you have a quicker and easier way to review before a quiz or an exam.

If you're a kinesthetic learner, note-taking can be helpful in focusing on the important information. Also, you may find having something small to keep your hands occupied during a lecture can help you stay focused.

Find out your learning style.

Beefing Up Your Study Skills

You may have developed excellent study habits in high school that will translate well to a college setting, but if you struggled in this area in high school, you'll have a whole new set of challenges in college. Expect that you'll need to adapt your way of studying because what worked for you in high school may not work in college. Even though we could write an entire book on effective study techniques and how we learn, for now we'll just look at some basic study habits that can be helpful to you.

Regularly review rather than cram. You can call this the best tip that few people take advantage of. It's proven that you need to review information several times before it moves from your short-term memory into your long-term memory. You might have classes that go on for eight weeks before you have a test! That's a lot of information that can show up on your midterm all of a sudden. So even though that midterm seems a long way off, you should start studying the very first day of class. Commit to reviewing your lecture notes and the written material at least twice per week. You'll want to do your review daily when you get within two weeks of an exam.

Participate in class. While participating might count as only 10 percent of your grade, participating does something else valuable for you. By getting involved in the discussion, you are making yourself an active learner. Participation requires you to listen, think, and then consolidate your thoughts enough to share your ideas. Those are all valuable parts of the learning process. Oh, and your effort in class will not go unnoticed by your professor!

Join a study group. If there are study groups popping up that you can join, do so. If there aren't any, create your own. Make your group effective by asking questions and reviewing not just the facts of the material but also the concepts surrounding those facts. It's more likely that you'll be asked to write an essay on the turning points that led to the Civil War than simply regurgitate a date or name.

Play teacher. Just as a good study group should ask questions about the material and the meaning and concepts behind it, you should do that even when you're studying alone. Don't just read the chapter; answer the questions that appear at the end. If there aren't many questions, imagine you were the professor and had to create an exam or essay question for the material. What might be asked? What concepts are critical? What is the author trying to say in the book? Obviously, the kinds of questions you ask will vary with the kinds of classes you're taking, but no matter what the material is, don't just read it — interact with it.

Find a good study spot. Don't study every subject you have in the same exact location. Try to vary where you study by having several different study spots so that you can keep your mind active. You may be surprised at how the location you study in can affect the material you're learning. You could be sitting at an exam and read a question and think, *I was reading that material when I was sitting on that bench* or *I was reviewing this at study group last week*.

Use flash cards. Flash cards aren't just for preschoolers. Flash cards can be especially helpful for kinesthetic learners (people who learn best by doing something physically). Take some key concepts or vocabulary words and put them on note cards. As you review them, be sure to explain the direct concept and also how it relates to the larger context of what you are studying.

Study out loud. For auditory learners (those who learn best by hearing), studying out loud can help in retaining the information. As you study a concept, close your eyes and talk through the concept out loud so that you can hear yourself. You can make adjustments as you go and can discover where the holes are in your learning when you stumble or struggle to connect two concepts.

Get quizzed. You can certainly quiz yourself throughout your study time, but if you have a friend you can grab to go through the material and ask you questions, that can be extremely beneficial. He or she might think of questions you haven't thought of at all. Then you can turn around and help that person study as well.

If you can, give yourself practice tests. For example, if you have a geography quiz, make a copy of the map and practice labeling things correctly before you have to do it in class.

As we said, a whole book can be written about study habits and how to improve them. The career planning office is usually a great resource for how to study effectively. Take advantage of all the help they are offering. It's up to you to put forth some specific effort to acquire the best tools for your academic success.

FROM THE TRENCHES

Don't underestimate the value of getting to know your professors face-to-face. Whether you're in a class of twenty or two hundred, take the time to talk to the professor. Ask questions, request advice, or simply get to know him or her personally. Later in life, that trusted professor or mentor might even be willing to be one of your references for graduate school or your first job.

About Cheating

The number of American students who engage in cheating and plagiarism has increased and colleges have had to step up their response to the problem.[1] Many students have come to believe that as long as they're not hurting anyone else, it's not really wrong. Professor Donald McCabe, leading expert in academic integrity, found that 70 percent of the university students surveyed admitted to cheating on exams and a whopping 84 percent cheated on writing assignments.[2]

Who's it really hurting? Well, you, for one! By not spending the time to learn, you are missing out on your own education. No, you may not be directly hurting other students in your class (unless you're hurting the grading curve), but you still lose. Your education is meant to prepare you for a future career. When you eventually have a job, you won't be getting tests, and you certainly won't be able to get the answers from your cheat sheet. That means you've got to be willing to do the hard work of learning and choosing not to cheat yourself.

When You're Having Trouble

If you are struggling to keep up with a class because you don't understand the concepts (or for any other reason), don't wait too long to speak up. The longer you wait, the further behind you'll fall. Every professor has office hours for students to come by and ask questions. Even if you just need to have something clarified, be sure to speak up. You may be able to ask quick questions before or after class, but for anything that might require a more in-depth answer, use the office hours and talk to your professor.

What if you've talked to the professor and you're still having trouble? That's when it's time to turn to a study group or on-campus tutoring. The extra cost of tutoring will be far less than having to retake a class.

FROM THE TRENCHES

TIP

Don't be afraid to talk with your professors if you have a problem. They like that you're showing initiative; plus, it's their job to help you.

It's Your Choice

College life will offer you so many opportunities, such as amazing classes and courses of study to choose from, the ability to study for a career that can eventually provide income for you and a family, and the chance to meet and interact with thoughtful and intelligent people. But with all of those opportunities come many choices.

We've already talked about how important it is to eat healthfully, exercise regularly, and get enough sleep. And we've also talked about some of the stuff that can actually harm you: smoking, drinking, using drugs, promiscuous behavior. All these are things that require regular choices from you. *Will I or won't I? What's best for me in this situation?*

And some choices are far easier than others. Even if we're tempted by something that is morally wrong or terrible for us, we are usually pretty clear that it's a "bad choice." Saying no to something that is clearly wrong—cheating on a test, stealing work, breaking the law—is pretty clear-cut.

Other times though, the choices you'll face won't have a clear right or wrong answer. *Should I live in the dorms or get an apartment next year? Should I take that class in the spring or fall? Should I major in voice performance or musical theater?* For those kinds of decisions, you'll have a lot of different things to take into consideration.

Hard Decisions

Unfortunately, many of the decisions you make to keep your mind and body healthy will require saying no to something else. Maybe you have to say no to hanging out and watching a movie because you need to finish a paper. It might mean you have to say no to going to that party because you know you'll be tempted to drink. Your schedule and the schedules of your friends may not always mesh, so if you find yourself having to bail on something so that you can concentrate on your studies, take charge of scheduling something fun when you do have the time. If saying no is the better choice, you can be strong and say no.

The Easy Way?

Making good choices that will help lead to a healthy life sometimes aren't the easiest choices. The easiest choices are usually the ones that aren't so great for us. If you go into school with the expectation and understanding that doing well in college will take discipline, focus, and hard work, you won't be surprised by the fact that it takes the same kind of tenacity with your decision making. Here are some examples of the "easier" things to do:

- Put off studying and just try to cram the night before the test.
- Bail on that 8 a.m. lecture and just try to get the notes from someone later.
- Let your friends talk you into doing anything but studying.

Those things might be easier, but you'll be missing out on so much more. Not only will you fail to get everything you can out of your college career but you may be wasting time on things that will end up being unimportant to you. It doesn't mean you can't have a social life or enjoy all of the amazing activities college has to offer. You should absolutely do those things! But you'll have to keep balance with what you choose to do and make sure your schooling is always one of your top priorities. The same kind of discipline it takes to choose what is good for you and your education is the kind you need for life.

Your Social Circles

In an earlier chapter, we looked at all the different places you might find friends and some of the clubs and activities you may involve yourself with. Before you settle too deeply into your different circles of friends, really look at who they are and how they might influence you. If the guys on your team are always talking about where to party, where might you find yourself if you choose to hang out with them? The attitudes and behaviors of those around you have the opportunity to rub off on you. It's a little bit like how a rock can be worn down by water. The water itself doesn't seem that strong, yet the constant flow of water over the rock eventually changes the rock's shape. That's what friends are like. Their ideas and opinions will keep washing over you, making it a short step to choosing things that might be harmful to your physical or spiritual health.

The best thing you can do for yourself is develop a strong "inner circle." A strong inner circle is made up of individuals who:

- Care about each other
- Want what's best for each other
- Value their education
- Value their own health and safety as well as the health and safety of their friends
- Share similar morals and beliefs
- Respect one another
- Encourage others to reach their full potential
- Speak the truth

That list is a pretty great description of who should be in anyone's inner circle. But if your spiritual health is important to you—and it should be!—then you'll want to add one more thing to that list: A healthy friend is going to be one who has an authentic and personal relationship with Jesus and has placed the importance of that relationship above everything else. We'll talk more about spiritual health in the next chapter, but for right now, let's just say that the spiritual makeup of that inner circle will be critical.

Can you be that kind of friend to others? If you can, you'll probably be able to find people who will be that kind of friend to you. Once you have a strong inner circle of friends, you can engage with the world and culture around you as an influencer instead of someone who is easily influenced by others.

A Question of Faith

It will probably come as no surprise to you that no matter what kind of college you go to, you will be surrounded by people who have varying levels of faith. (In the next chapter, we'll talk in more detail about spiritual health.) And if you choose a secular college or university, not only will you encounter Christians of varying faith levels but you'll also encounter a wide range of cultures and religions. While a university will have multiple Christian fellowship groups for you to be a part of, it may also have groups for Jewish, Muslim, Buddhist, and even atheist students. And that's just other students. Your professors will have their own religious perspectives that may not coincide with Christian beliefs.

When Derrick objected to an assignment that required him to view a theater production with highly sexualized content, his professor's response was one of derision. Even though Derrick offered to see a different production at his own expense, he was subjected to ridicule of his beliefs and accused of not being able to handle the real world. Derrick's story is just one example of many. Your belief system will undergo challenges from every angle. How will you deal with that?

Let's be honest: You may be going into college questioning your own beliefs. There are a number of great resources to check out if you're struggling, including *Evidence That Demands a Verdict*, by Josh McDowell, and *The Case for Christ*, by Lee Strobel. Strobel actually has several books that may be helpful to you as you seek to figure out what you believe.

The thing not to do is simply reject God and assume you've already figured Him out. We could each spend a lifetime pursuing Him and never come to fully understand who He is.

Other Belief Systems

Honestly, you could take several semesters of classes on world religions and still not fully comprehend the nuances of each kind of religious expression you might encounter at school. Therefore, going into an overview of them is really meant to give you a basic framework to help you understand how they differ from Christianity.

Baha'i Faith
The Baha'i faith is essentially monotheistic and they believe that Bha'u'llah is the latest divine messenger. He is believed to be in the same category as Abraham, Moses, Buddha, Krishna, Jesus Christ, and Mohammed. Central to their faith is that humanity is

one single race, meant to be united as one global society. Their basic teachings include, among others, an "abandonment of all forms of prejudice, assurance to women of full equality, the elimination of poverty and wealth and the recognition of the unity and relativity of religious truth."[3]

There are many ideas contained within their teachings that are very appealing to today's culture. Who would argue against eliminating poverty or the importance of universal education? But many ideas and teachings from the Baha'i faith contradict Scripture. The main conflict with Christianity is that Jesus was not simply a Divine Messenger; He is the Son of God.

Buddhism

Buddhism is a religion practiced by about 300 million people, and while it is most prevalent in such countries as Thailand and China, it is becoming increasingly popular in Western societies. It began 2,500 years ago and is centered around the "enlightenment" of Siddhartha Gautama, known as Buddha. The basic philosophy is threefold: "to live a moral life, to be mindful and aware of thoughts and actions and to develop wisdom and understanding."[4] In essence, people of this faith believe that following those principles will "lead to true happiness." They do not worship Buddha or claim that he was a god, although they do pay reverence to his image. Buddhists are tolerant of all other belief systems and do not seek to preach or convert. The idea of karma—that every cause has an effect—comes from Buddhism. It is also rather open-ended and is not necessarily a fixed menu of beliefs. Adherents are encouraged to seek their own paths.

Here again, we have principles that are good things overall, but the core idea is that the purpose of life is happiness and the path to true happiness exists within ourselves. The Bible gives a much different picture of man, our depravity, and the need for redemption and salvation through Christ.

Hinduism

Hinduism is also known as Sanatana Dharma, or "Eternal Way," and claims to be the planet's oldest religion. Hindus believe in one "pervasive Supreme Being" but also believe that divine beings exist in "unseen worlds," so their temple rituals seek a communion with those other "devas and gods." They believe in karma as well and that people are reincarnated over and over until they reach "god realization." Hindus believe that no religion teaches a way to salvation that is above another and that essentially "all paths lead to god's light."[5]

There are similarities to Buddhism here and it contradicts many of the basic and core tenants of Christianity. While Hinduism promotes the belief that we are made holy as we get reincarnated over and over, the Bible teaches that man dies once. We don't get multiple chances to get it right. Our only hope for holiness and a relationship with God is Jesus.

Islam

You'd be hard-pressed to find someone who has not heard of Islam, but not many people could really explain what it is. There is no doubt that the practice of Islam is growing, and the population of Muslims (those who practice Islam) is said to be around

1.5 billion worldwide.[6] They are monotheistic, which means they believe in one god and that Mohammed was a prophet who was given a divine message that is known as the Holy Quran. People who practice Islam live by five pillars, which are focused on paying alms, a pilgrimage to Mecca, fasting during Ramadan, daily prayers, and witnessing to others that Allah should be worshipped and that Mohammed was his prophet. Islam recognizes many of the Old Testament prophets and places Jesus in the category of prophet rather than Son of God. There are several different branches of Islam, so the exact practices and customs vary between the sects.[7]

Unfortunately, it would take a whole book to compare Christianity and Islam, so we'll outline just a few of the main theological errors Christians should know.

Beliefs of Islam	Beliefs of Christianity
Jesus is a prophet.	Jesus is the Son of God (see Matthew 16:16).
People are born pure.	All of us are sinners (see Romans 3:23; Psalm 51:5).
We can draw near to Allah through sincerity and worship.	Only through Christ can we be restored to God (see John 14:6; Hebrews 4:14-16).
The Quran is inspired by Allah (through the prophet Mohammed).	The Bible is inerrant and complete and nothing can be added to it (see Revelation 22:18).
There is no God but Allah.	God is revealed in three persons: Father, Son, and Holy Spirit.

While this is just a sampling, there are many Islamic beliefs that directly contradict Christianity.

Sikhism

Sikhism was founded more than five hundred years ago and claims to have more than two million followers worldwide. While it has some similarities to Hinduism and Buddhism (the soul goes through cycles of birth and death and the end goal is to merge with god), it also has some big differences in that its followers condemn such rituals as fasting, pilgrimages, and renunciation of the world. They preach that everyone is equal and the goal of life is to "lead an exemplary existence so that one may merge with god." Their teachings are culled from the teachings of ten gurus, and they believe that there is one god who is the same for all people and all religions.[8]

Do you see how this idea of universalism (all roads lead to god) keeps coming up in many of these world religions? It's important for you to be able to distinguish where the errors in these teachings are according to Scripture.

Taoism

Taoism, most closely identified with the yin-yang symbol that is used even in the United States, is a religion that gleans its philosophy from a book of poems called the *Tao Te Ching*. It teaches that the physical, mental, and metaphysical realms (what Christians would call spiritual) are meant to all be unified. Their main goal is "contentment," and they believe that can be achieved by following their nine principles.[9]

Those who follow Tao are expected to spend much energy on seeking oneness within themselves and the development of their own mind, body, and spirit in order to achieve contentment. Therefore, they are encouraged to not get involved with anything that doesn't have "tangible personal benefits." It's probably the most inward-focused of all the religions and clearly is a direct contradiction to most facets of Christianity.

Unitarian Universalism

This religion is included here because you are very likely to run across it if you haven't already. More and more people are joining this religion, and although many think it's just another church, its teaching directly defies the Scriptures.

In essence, it's a religious community that encourages all of its members to "seek their own spiritual path." They draw some of their teachings from Christianity and Judaism but also from humanism, paganism, and other world religions. Basically, everything and everyone is accepted and there are no prescribed tenants they are expected to accept other than ideals such as compassion, equality, justice, and love.[10] These are noble ideals, to be sure, and ones Jesus Himself talked about at length; however, the clear danger is that the religion's followers reject the core parts of Christianity, namely, that Jesus Christ was God, He died on the cross to redeem mankind, and it is only through His sacrifice that we can be forgiven of our sins and have fellowship with God.

Atheism

American atheists claim that 15 percent (or 50 million) of Americans are atheists.[11] What does that mean? Atheists deny the existence of a god or gods of any kind. As a group, they tend to be politically invested and organize themselves primarily to fight for their own civil liberties and the complete separation of church and state.

Agnostics

Unlike atheists, who deny the existence of any god or deity, agnostics choose to neither believe nor disbelieve in any kind of deity or god. T. H. Huxley is credited for defining the term and believed that we would never be able to know for sure about the origin of the universe or the involvement of a deity.[12] The terms *atheist* and *agnostic* are related, though, and the line that separates them is quite thin. An agnostic may be slightly more open to empirical evidence than an atheist, but both approach the concept of God with much skepticism and, at times, hostility.

Deism

Those who call themselves deist do so with a clear definition of what that means. Deism teaches that a creator or god exists but that we know so not because of faith but because of reason. Basically, followers say that you can look at the "laws and designs of nature" and reasonably conclude that there is an intelligent design to the universe. However, they also outright reject the notion that God is involved with people on a national or personal level and insist that divine revelations or messengers, such as Jesus and the prophets, are the stuff of fairy tales.[13]

Many people actually fall under the "deism" definition whether or not they would personally identify themselves as such.

Nonreligious (Secular)

The number of Americans who identify themselves as nonreligious is placed at around 38 million.[14] We really have no way of knowing how accurate that is because even those who might classify themselves as Christians could feasibly fall into this same category in practice. Those who are nonreligious may have rejected organized religion but still have some sort of belief system or they may function much like an agnostic (deciding that they won't decide). You will likely run across many people on a college campus who fall under this category.

Neo-Paganism, Wicca, and Witchcraft

Neo-paganism and the related belief systems of witchcraft and Wicca are very difficult to define because even among people who call themselves neo-pagans or druids or witches, you'll find a wide disparity of definitions. So for our purposes here, we'll define a few of the commonalities, but you need to understand that this movement is highly undefined in general. It's probably easiest to think of paganism as the umbrella term, with many of the other belief systems falling underneath it in some way. Here are some of the common elements of the wide variety of pagan practices:

- A belief in powers and forces that are active in the world today, often worshipped as gods and goddesses, making it primarily a polytheistic belief system
- Highly focused on nature, natural elements, and harmony with nature
- Have a wide variety of ceremonies for worship, entreating powers, and harmony in nature
- Very flexible sets of beliefs that can incorporate modern elements with ancient beliefs

- May or may not incorporate the practice of magic and witchcraft (the idea being that not all pagans are witches but most witches can be considered pagans)
- May even incorporate elements from Judaism, Christianity, and other major religious forms

Paganism is not a well-defined set of beliefs; instead, it is more a buffet of options that each person can pick and choose from as they wish. Wicca is a more defined segment of paganism and includes several guidelines for the practice that are expected to be followed within that community.

The most concerning part of neo-paganism is that it basically encourages its adherents to create their own system of beliefs, with no accountability or responsibility. Most people who become pagans and witches do so during their teens and early twenties, so it is a practice that is sought after by the very age group you will fall within during college. It is likely something you will run across.

Encountering those who consider themselves pagans, druids, or witches requires the same kind of love and compassion you would need for someone who was nonreligious or a Buddhist. People are wonderfully unique and varied, and although we wanted to define the categories a bit, people are often not so easy to figure out. But hopefully you will see where some beliefs and ideas might be coming from so that you can more confidently talk about your own beliefs.

Free download about worldviews from NavPress

How to Respond to People of Other Faiths

So what will you do when you run across a professing atheist in your geography class or discover that your professor is a devout Muslim? What if you discover that your next-door neighbor considers herself a pagan? It could happen. And even if it doesn't happen during school, it could happen at a job or summer internship.

Before Jesus ascended, He gave us what has come to be known as the Great Commission. He said,

> God authorized and commanded me to commission you: Go out and train everyone you meet, far and near, in this way of life, marking them by baptism in the threefold name: Father, Son, and Holy Spirit. Then instruct them in the practice of all I have commanded you. I'll be with you as you do this, day after day after day, right up to the end of the age. (Matthew 28:19)

Sharing the gospel with others is something all believers are supposed to be doing. For some, that is an easier thing to do than for others. Some are naturally extroverted or eloquent with their words. It might be easy to think you can just leave it up to that kind of person to try to influence your campus and share who Jesus is with others. But each one of us should be taking the opportunities the Lord gives us. You can truly be a leader and influence others no matter who you are.

Here are a few things to keep in mind as you seek to be a leader and influencer on your campus.

Your Life Witness

A lot of preachers talk about how the way you live your life is its own witness; the power of a life submitted to Christ cannot be underestimated. If you truly love and follow the Lord, your life should look different. Notice that we said "different," not "perfect." No one's life is perfect, and Christians face sorrows and trials just like the rest of the world. But we should respond to things differently when we are living out what the Bible says.

Let's say that you discover that your roommate has been complaining about you behind your back. You have lots of options. Some might respond by complaining about him to others. Some might get angry and ignore him. Some might instigate an argument with accusations. But Christians have another option. In Matthew, we discover how we should deal with a problem like this: "If a fellow believer hurts you, go and tell him—work it out between the two of you. If he listens, you've made a friend" (18:15). That may resolve the problem, but even if it doesn't, we are also asked to forgive one another of sins (see Colossians 3:13). If you choose to deal with life by looking at what God has asked us to do in the Scriptures, with His help your life can look radically different. It can be hard, and that's why it is such an amazing witness.

Let's say it's your professor who doesn't believe in God. Do you think you'd be able to show your professor something about Jesus if you choose to be a punctual, respectful, and diligent student? What if your work was poor, you were always late, and you didn't put forth real effort in the class? Your attitude and behavior toward others affects how much influence and weight your words might carry.

The Importance of Listening and Observing

Before we can engage someone in really talking about Jesus or the gospel message, we should take the time to find out what they believe. Ask questions! Find out what their thoughts are. What did their parents believe? How do they feel about God and why? If we truly listen to others, we can figure out where the real issues lie. When we take the time to listen, other people will be more open to listening to our views too. Maybe they believe in God but don't think He has anything to do with their individual lives. Well, that's something you can talk about! Once you start to understand how other people are thinking about spiritual things, the better you can help focus the conversation.

Study

You do not have to be some Bible scholar to speak about God and His Word. However, the more you know about what's in the Bible, the better able you will be to respond to others' needs. For instance, if you know that the guy in your class is a neo-pagan, you should know the basics about what he believes and what Scriptures show the problems with that belief system. Asking great questions will reveal how a person thinks about spiritual issues, and if you know the Word, you'll know exactly what to say. But you have to have the Word inside of you in order for it to come out at the right time.

Testimony

We all have a testimony. Your testimony is the story of how you came to follow the Lord. Even if you've followed Him since you were little, you still probably have a story to share about how God helped you through a difficult time or showed Himself to you in a powerful way. Take a few minutes to write down your story. It should be short enough that you can tell it to someone in five minutes or less. Talk about what your life was like before you trusted Christ, why and how you chose to trust Him, and what your life has been like since you made your decision. You can even include relevant Bible verses. Your personal story is of great value, so if you get the chance, share it! You never know what questions or conversations may come up because of it.

Compassion or Conversion?

When Christians show genuine care and concern for people, it's always more effective than simply going out to try and convert others. Take the time to get to know the people around you. Show care and concern. Pray for them. Serve them. Help out where you can. Then, when you do get the chance to share the gospel, your words will carry far more weight because others will have seen your love in action and know they are not just one more soul you're trying to save.

So with all of the choices, decisions, and people you will encounter at school, do you see how important it is to keep your mind healthy and develop an inner circle of people you can trust? The truth is that you won't be able to navigate everything by your own strength and understanding. We get to see a small portion of the big picture. Even more important than keeping your mind and body healthy is the state of your spiritual health.

11

Spiritual Health

Our spiritual health is inextricably tied to our emotional and physical health. Let's take an in-depth look at gauging where your spiritual health is right now and learn how to strengthen yourself spiritually so that you have the tools and advantages you need to succeed in school.

Your spiritual health is a lot like your immune system. If you are spiritually weak, you will be more susceptible to the lure and deceptions the world will offer. If you are spiritually strong, you'll be quick to recognize those deceptions and walk away from them. Those temptations will be offered from every angle. We've talked about some of them already:

- Physical temptations to engage in unhealthy behavior or not take care of yourself in ways that honor the body God gave you

- Mental temptations to not value the education you're being offered or not discipline yourself to do hard work and instead cut corners to make it easier

But along with those will be spiritual temptations and many different experiences and opinions, such as:

- The guy on your lacrosse team who "tried church" once but now thinks organized religion is stupid
- The girl down the hall who calls herself a Christian but parties every weekend, doesn't bother with school, and basically does whatever she wants
- The guy who ridicules you for even having a Bible, much less reading it

While you may encounter those kinds of guys and girls, you can handle the situation if you are serious about keeping yourself spiritually healthy. No matter what kind of school you attend, your college experience can include amazing spiritual growth, and you usually don't have to look too far to find it. Oh, you may have to visit a few different organizations or churches to find that perfect fit, but with such a wide variety available on most campuses, you can make great spiritual progress while you're earning your degree.

Your Spiritual Health Meter

Where would you rate your spiritual health right now? Healthy? Unhealthy? Nonexistent? Go ahead and be brutally honest with yourself. Let's start with a little quiz, but promise to be honest. You don't have to write the answers here in the book; if you'd rather, get a separate piece of paper to write your answers on and throw it away if you're worried about someone finding it.

We get this funny idea that we can hide things from God. Adam and Eve tried to hide from God after they sinned in the garden. It's even mentioned in Psalm 139:7-8:

> Is there anyplace I can go to avoid your Spirit?
>> to be out of your sight?
> If I climb to the sky, you're there!
>> If I go underground, you're there!

We have this natural (though dangerous) urge to hide when we know we are being dishonest with others and with God. So take off any masks you've been hiding behind and really search your heart.

Rate these statements on a scale of 1 to 5:

1 (not true) 2 (a little true) 3 (somewhat true)
4 (very true) 5 (incredibly true)

_____ 1. I believe that God and His Son, Jesus, are both real.

_____ 2. I believe that God knows more about life than I do.

_____ 3. I believe that God cares about my life.

_____ 4. I believe that God cares about the decisions I make.

_____ 5. I believe that God wants me to live a certain way.

_____ 6. I want to please God.

_____ 7. I believe that God is good.

_____   8. I believe that God has a plan for my life.

_____   9. I believe that I can be forgiven of my sins.

_____ 10. I believe that the Bible is true and still relevant for my life today.

_____ 11. I feel that I know who God is.

_____ 12. I feel that I can hear from God.

_____ 13. I believe that my faith in God is strong.

All right, now take a look at your numbers. If you have mostly 4s and 5s, you're probably solid in your faith and willing to seek ways to continue growing spiritually during college. That's great! Everything we'll talk about is as true for you as someone who might be questioning his or her faith. And you never know when you'll encounter other Christians who are unsure about some of these things. You might be able to pray for and encourage them as they seek to grow spiritually stronger.

If you have a lot of 1s, 2s, or 3s, you are probably feeling a bit unsure not only about God but also where He fits into your life. You might even be questioning if God is even real or if He really cares about you at all. If that's you, would you be willing to try an experiment? Would you be willing to give a relationship with God another try during college? Would you be willing to let go of any hurt or anger toward God, ask Him to forgive you, and start fresh? If you're willing, here's a prayer you can say right now as a starting point:

Dear Lord, I'm feeling very unsure about You right now. I'm feeling _____ [hurt, confused, lost, lonely] and I just don't feel as though You have listened to me. But I'm willing to realize that maybe I'm the one who hasn't really been listening. I'm sorry for _____ [my anger, rejecting You, ignoring You]. Please forgive me. I ask You to cleanse me of my pride, my anger, my selfishness — anything that would get in the way of my really hearing from You and understanding who You are. Help me to seek You with all of my heart. I ask that You would help me believe that You love me, that You care for me, and that You have a plan for my life. In Jesus' name, amen.

If you prayed that, we encourage you to let someone (a friend, a parent, a trusted advisor) know that you want to seriously pursue God. Ask the person to pray for you and check in with you now and then about how it's going. And once you get to school, be quick about getting into relationships with other believers. We'll explore that a bit more in depth right now.

Getting Involved with Other Believers

Remember how we talked about that "inner circle"? If you are a believer, your inner circle should include several other strong believers. If someone does not share our faith in God, our relationship with the person is limited. That inner circle for you should include various types of believers, but typically a non-believer needs to be in one of your outer circles. You may have great opportunities to interact with the person, but that's not the kind of person you should go to for advice or support. Your inner circle should be a safe place to seek help, encouragement, support, and truth.

Maturity Levels

As Christians, we should seek to have three different kinds of relationships, as all three are important. The first is with a trusted advisor. Advisors are those who are ahead of us spiritually and we can look to for solid, prayerful advice, encouragement, and support. They'll give us honest feedback about things they see in our lives. Although an advisor is typically someone a bit older, it's not necessarily about age but rather about their commitment and maturity. You may find someone your age who is a very mature believer. Or you may find an upperclassman, teacher, or ministry leader on campus who can fulfill that role.

The second kind of relationship is a peer relationship. These are people who are close to where you are at in your spiritual maturity. Peers can walk, pray, encourage, and support one another in many ways. The best kinds of peer relationships are ones in which you can hold each other accountable if there's a problem and challenge one another to grow deeper in your relationships with God. Whether you have many or only a few of these kinds of friends, these peer relationships are important.

The third kind of relationship is a mentoring relationship. Having a relationship with someone who is either brand new to his or her faith or just getting started can be very valuable to both of you. This is when you have a chance to mentor others in their faith and become a role model to those around you. You may even find yourself in the role of trusted advisor! Not only is this a wonderful relationship to be able to cultivate but it can be very motivating to you spiritually when you know that others are watching you and learning about God through your behavior.

Missionary Dating

Don't do it. Really, that's all that needs to be said. But in case you're unsure about what "missionary dating" is, let's define it. Basically, it's when a Christian chooses to date a nonbeliever, thinking that nonbeliever will be influenced to become a believer. The term *nonbeliever* can also include those who are essentially agnostic, meaning they don't disagree with the principles of Christianity but they don't fully agree with them either.

When you "missionary date," you are essentially pulling a nonbeliever into that "inner circle." If someone doesn't share your most core beliefs, you cannot have a thriving relationship. Plus, you'll be much more likely to compromise your beliefs when you're receiving counsel and advice that isn't backed up by the Word of God.

If your faith is essential to you, protecting that inner circle is vital, especially in dating relationships.

Your Roommate

You may be allowed to pick your roommate, but as an incoming student, you may not know anyone to pick. It's likely the university has a system that matches incoming students with each other and pairs them into assigned rooms. Your best bet in that case is to make sure your paperwork is thoroughly filled out. For example, you've already gotten into school, but there's a spot to list your activities and interests. Well, that may be a section the college uses to pair people up, so fill out everything with as much information as you can. You are also probably allowed to opt out of answering anything about your faith, but include it because that may be used in pairing you with someone too.

Keep in mind that some people who identified themselves as Christians on the paperwork may have been expected to put that down (by a parent) or they may have simply assumed that's what they are because they aren't Jewish or Muslim. You won't really know anything about who they are until you meet them and interact with them. They may end up becoming a close friend or maybe not. That's okay. You might have to look beyond your roommates and suitemates for your inner circle.

If you can request a roommate, you may want to go to the Youth Transition Network's site, www.LiveAbove.com. The site is all about trying to help Christians connect with other believers and ministries at a new school. You might be able to connect with possible roommates and find out about organizations you might be interested in becoming a part of. The site also has online articles, videos, and resources about how to plug in with God, other believers, and campus ministries while away at school.

Campus Ministries

College campuses have a wide array of ministries you can get involved with. Many ministries have a mix of small-group Bible studies, large-group meetings, mission trip opportunities, and leadership training and conferences. The exact flavor of each group may vary not only group to group but also campus to campus. Remember that organizations are made up of individuals and you might simply click better with one group than another, so be willing to try out several before you make up your mind about which one to focus on. Getting involved in a campus ministry group can go a long way toward helping you develop your inner circle, grow spiritually, and involve yourself with missionary or leadership opportunities.

We'll take a quick look at some of the national organizations that maintain chapters at different campuses in the United States and abroad.

The Navigators

The Navigators collegiate ministry has staff at more than 100 colleges and universities around the nation, and another 62 campuses have a volunteer ministry group known as NavFusion. The Navigators' mission is to know Christ and make Him known, and they seek to encourage students to grow deeper in their faith through Bible study, mentorship, and disciple-ship. They build a strong community through weekly meetings, conferences, and summer training programs across the nation. To learn more about The Navigators and see if they have a group on your campus, check out their website at www.navigators.org/us/ministries/college.

The Navigators

InterVarsity Christian Fellowship

InterVarsity may sound like an intramural sports club, but it's really a vibrant ministry that exists on more than 550 campuses around the nation. There's a pretty good chance you'll find this ministry at your school. They have a vision to see students and faculty transformed, campuses renewed, and world changers developed. They minister to students through large-group weekly meetings, smaller Bible study groups, leadership training, discipleship, conferences, and events. In addition, they have useful online

InterVarsity

materials such as Bible studies and videos. To find out more about InterVarsity or see if there's a chapter on your campus, go to www.intervarsity.org.

Cru (Campus Crusade for Christ International)

Cru is a huge ministry with a presence in 191 countries, but their focus on campuses has never waned. Their vision is to help launch and build movements of spiritual multiplication so that everyone will know someone who truly follows Jesus Christ. The ministry efforts of Cru exist on more than 1,000 campuses across the United States and beyond. Cru offers weekly meetings, small-group Bible studies, mission projects, and conferences. To find out more, go to http://campuscrusadeforchrist.com.

Cru

Fellowship of Christian Athletes (FCA)

The Fellowship of Christian Athletes is a ministry that is active from middle school through high school and college, so if you've already participated with FCA in your own community, you may want to continue your involvement on campus. It is led by athletes and coaches with a mission and desire to share the gospel of Jesus Christ with the lost and to seek to grow and mature followers of Jesus Christ. If you love Jesus and sports, it's a great place to get involved. Their website is http://fcacampus101.com/college.

FCA

Denominational and Church-Based Ministries

Although the ministries we've already discussed are not affiliated with any particular denomination, many denominations will have a group or presence on your campus. In addition, specific churches in the immediate area of your college may run a campus ministry as well.

The best way to find out what's available on your campus is to look on your school's website in the student life section. You'll be able to access a list of everything that's available, and you can start narrowing down the organizations you want to visit.

Choosing a Church

Closely related to finding a campus ministry to connect with is trying to find a local church to become a part of. You might think,

I'm doing all of these other Christian meetings; why do I need to go to church, too? Good question!

First, connecting with a local body of believers allows you to interact with and get to know people from all phases of life. At school, nearly everyone is around the same age and has had similar life experiences. But at a local church, you'll find young couples, singles, families, older couples, and everything in between. It can help you get perspective about how following God can be dynamic and wonderful no matter what age you are.

Second, a local church may be able to bless you in unexpected ways. Usually the churches around college campuses have special programs for college students. Church members may provide transportation for you from campus. They may connect you with a local host family who can provide a place of encouragement and blessing while you're away from home. It may be a place to find trusted advisors who will pray for you and support you.

Third, being part of a local body knits you into the community. It's likely that your campus will be your home for four years or longer, so settling in and finding a church to be part of can make it feel more like home.

You should be able to get a list of local churches (including ones that provide transportation) from your student life office or website. You may need to try a few out before you find that right fit.

TIP

FROM THE TRENCHES

Find a good church to attend. I cannot express how important it is to keep going to church every Sunday. It's so much easier to get lost in college if you don't have a community of people to support you. You need to keep feeding your spirit in order to stay strong.

Social Christianity

The one caution about getting heavily involved with campus ministry activities and completely surrounding yourself with other believers is that some people can move into a kind of social Christianity. If you're hanging out with Christians, living with Christians, and going to Christian meetings, you end up sounding and looking just like a Christian because that's who you're with all the time. This isn't necessarily a bad thing, but true Christianity isn't about what you look like during worship or how much Scripture you know; it's about having an interactive relationship between you and God. That "you and God" time still has to be the priority over all the other campus meetings you attend. What does your faith look like when no one else is around? That's the kind of faith that will carry you through tough times and help you know how to draw near to God and seek His wisdom.

Enjoy the great meetings and Bible studies — they can be really wonderful! But don't let God ever become just a "social group" thing. Take time to make sure you're unplugging from everything (and everyone) else so you can get time to really plug in with God.

Building Your Faith

Let's turn our attention now to that "you and God" issue. You might hear great speakers on campus, you might get the chance to go to a great conference, and you might have a great weekly Bible study group. Those things are all going to feed you spiritually, but you cannot be completely dependent on having others tell you what God says. You must become adept at searching God's Word, hearing His voice, and discovering what He is saying to you personally.

Look at it this way: Say you have two different classes, Spirit Class and World Class. You spend a lot of time on World Class. You go to every lecture. You talk about it with the other students. You look for ways to do extra projects for World Class. You even start a study group so that you can spend more time on it. How do you think you'll do in World Class? You'll probably do quite well. But the Spirit Class isn't the same. You go now and then. Every once in a while, there's a cool lecture, but you don't seem to remember it. Your professor keeps asking to talk to you, but you keep ditching him. It's not a bad class, but sometimes you think it's not worth it to go because you've fallen too far behind. What kind of grade would you get in Spirit Class? Probably not a good one.

Your spiritual health is not something that's naturally either hot or cold. We make it hot or cold depending on how much time, energy, and attention we give it. Just like your classes, if you don't put the time in, you won't learn or grow in your faith. It's pretty straightforward. Likewise, if you don't spend time becoming spiritually strong, when the tests and temptations come, you won't have the strength needed to resist.

How do you become spiritually stronger? Let's look at some of the things we can do to not only strengthen ourselves in the Lord but also more deeply get to know God and hear His voice.

Staying in the Word

The Bible is one of the greatest treasures we have as Christians. The Scriptures help us come to know who God is and how He's worked in the lives of humans to redeem us from sin. It's a pretty amazing story. But what's even more amazing is that no matter how many times we read the Bible, God can show us something new about Himself each time.

The Bible is also critical to helping us tell the difference between what God says about something and what the world says about it. The popular opinions of our culture can sometimes sound good and reasonable, but there's no way for us to know if they are true unless we compare the world's ideas with what Scripture actually says. Learning to do that regularly can help us navigate the cultural waters without sinking. But even more than that, you may hear Christians say things that don't line up with the Word of God, and the more you know the Word, the more quickly you'll recognize those kinds of errors.

There are two types of Bible reading, and both have value. Usually, our best bet is to incorporate both kinds into our daily study habits.

Bible Reading

The first kind of Bible reading is just that: reading. Every. Single. Day. It's not enough to glance at the Bible here and there; we have to read it every day. One of the best ways to do this is to use a Bible reading plan and read through the whole Bible. Even if you've done this before, it is a great way to get a perspective on the entire Word. There are many Bible reading plans to choose from, but we recommend using one in which you read a few chapters from the Old Testament and some of the New Testament each day. It's usually a manageable amount and can be broken up so one portion is read in the morning and the other before bed. But you should choose a plan that works best for you and then stick with it.

The Internet has dozens of different plans you can print out and tuck in your Bible, but nowadays there are reading plan apps that you can download onto your phone to keep track of your reading. See the "Bible Reading Plans" section on pages 196–197 for a list of websites.

Find your Bible reading plan at YouVersion.

Bible Study

The second kind of Bible reading is when you study it more deeply on your own. If you can find a great small-group Bible study, you can use what you're studying in the group as a springboard for your own personal study in between meetings. That can be a great way to interact with other believers about the same topics and ideas.

Some people may not know how to really study the Bible, and if that describes you, don't let anything stop you from jumping in and learning just how much there is to discover in the Word of God. Here is a quick look at some of the different approaches you can take.

Topics. You can focus on a topic that is either an issue you might be facing or just something you want to know more about. You might choose to study what the Bible has to say about pride, sex, anger, selfishness, or maybe even what Jesus said or the parables He taught. You can use a resource such as Bible Gateway (www .biblegateway.com) or a concordance (a book that lists every word in the Bible and every place that word appears) to look up your topic.

People. You can also choose a character introduced in Scripture and study his or her choices and decisions and what God's purpose was for the person. The stories contained in the Scriptures of people's lives are rich with wisdom on how God intercedes and guides those who belong to Him.

Books of the Bible. You can take one book of the Bible and study it verse by verse to discover the history of the book, information about the writer God inspired to pen it, and the themes and topics the book covers. Each book of the Bible provides a very different experience.

Bible resources. Here are some resources that can be very useful for really digging into the Word:

- A good concordance
- Multiple translations (for looking up the same Scripture in more than one version)

- A Bible dictionary
- Commentaries
- A biblical atlas
- A topical index

Now, that could end up being quite a lot of books, but you can actually find most of these resources right online. The Bible Study Tools website (www.biblestudytools.com) allows you to search and explore all kinds of resources you can use for your own study or a group study. It even has an online devotional (a daily reading with a key verse used), several Bible reading plans, and dozens of translations. So if you're not really sure where to start, this website is a pretty good place to explore.

Published studies. Even though studying the Bible on your own and learning to use the resources we described earlier are very valuable, there is a lot to be learned from gifted teachers and the Bible studies they publish. There is a huge variety to choose from! Some focus on topics or people from the Bible, others are geared toward certain phases of life (such as being single) or a certain gender, and still others are focused on helping new believers understand critical foundational principles.

If there is a Christian bookstore nearby, you might find something that sparks your interest right on the shelves. But that's going to represent only a small portion of what's available. Both NavPress (www.th1nkbooks.com) and LifeWay (www.lifeway.com) have a great variety of studies, but you can also search www.ChristianBook.com to find many more choices.

What's great about published studies is that you're able to learn valuable things but not have to spend quite as much time figuring out where to go next. If you find something interesting, you can also share it with a small group or friend. Being able to chat with someone about what you're learning not only makes it more fun but also gives you a different perspective.

Scripture Memory

The Bible is truly filled with great wisdom and advice for all types of situations. No, it doesn't come right out and tell you whether or not you should date, and you won't be able to find a verse that tells you what your major should be, but the Lord absolutely uses Scriptures to lead us in the right direction. The more we know of what is in the Word and actually have it tucked away inside our heads, the quicker the Holy Spirit can bring a relevant Scripture to mind when we need it.

But if it's not already inside of us, it won't be able to come out of us. The Bible can seem a bit overwhelming for some, but rest assured that you don't need to memorize the whole thing for memorization to be useful to you.

You can pull out verses that are meaningful to you and start there, adding to your collection as you complete daily Bible readings and studies. Or you can use a system such as the *Topical Memory System*, which contains verse cards and a workbook to help you

Verseminder for your phone

memorize Scripture. There's even an electronic version of the system called *Verseminder*, which can be used on Windows or a Mac. *Verseminder* can help you improve your knowledge of the Bible and track your progress as you become more proficient.

Evaluating Your Motives

You can read the Bible all day long, memorize it, and study it, but unless you're approaching it with an attitude of wanting to know what God thinks and who He is, you may not get anything out of it. When we approach any spiritual discipline (prayer, Bible reading, memorization) as simply a way to check something off our spiritual checklists, we're missing out on that deep interaction with God that we all need. Anytime you approach Bible study, time with God, or prayer, be sure to focus yourself. Ask God to help you have wisdom and understanding and to show you the things you need to understand about Him and yourself.

Spending Time with God

When you go hang out with a friend, what do you do? Do you sit down, talk about all your problems, beg the person to help you fix things, and then walk away? Probably not. And if you did, your friend might not want to hang out with you very often! Obviously, spending time with God will be different from spending time with a friend; after all, one of the things God calls us to do is worship, and we definitely don't worship a friend. But, in a sense, our relationship with God and our interactions with Him should be similar to any other relationship we might have. When we get to know people and become close friends, we learn what they like, what they hate, what they love, how they think, and what's important to them. Those are the same things we can discover about God as we study His Word and spend time with Him.

But what does it mean to spend time with God? How do you go about hanging out with the God of the universe? Well, by dying on the cross, Jesus made a way for us to have a real relationship with God. There is no magic formula, and it's not some four-step process to get what we want. However, the Bible does give us some great things to keep in mind as we approach our time with Him.

Worship and Thanksgiving

Over and over in Scripture, we are called to worship God, give Him praise, and be thankful. He is the God of the whole universe and wants to spend time with us. That's a pretty amazing thought. When we worship God, it reminds us of just how awesome He is and all that we have to be thankful for. Human beings have a tendency to be pretty selfish. We want what we don't have, and we can easily get into a mindset of feeling as though we deserve something from God. So that's why worship and thanksgiving are so powerful. Worship reminds us who we are talking to, and thanksgiving reminds us of how much He's already done for us. It can help us have the right attitude.

One of the best things you can do is begin keeping a book of remembrance in which you can record your own history with the

Lord. You can use a physical journal, an app on your phone, or a file you create in your computer. You can keep it like a regular list or write short paragraphs if you want to elaborate on anything. Whatever works for you! Begin recording everything God does for you. Write down what He shows you in the Word or when He answers a prayer. List the blessings He has given you. You don't have to sit down and try to re-create everything you've ever experienced. Just start with today, and then add in other things as you remember and think about them. You can use this list as encouragement when you go through something tough. And we all do from time to time. But if we can stay focused on all God has already done, we'll be better able to trust Him to take care of us no matter what it is we're facing.

Another idea is to create a Daily Three. Before you start your time with God, think about three things you can be grateful to God for. You can even write them down and record them in your book of remembrance.

Repentance

In the same way that worship and thanksgiving get us in the right frame of mind for prayer, repentance is also a critical part of the time we spend with God. Jesus talked about the issue of forgiveness in Matthew when He said, "In prayer there is a connection between what God does and what you do. You can't get forgiveness from God, for instance, without also forgiving others. If you refuse to do your part, you cut yourself off from God's part" (6:14-15). God cannot forgive us unless we're willing to forgive others. So when you settle down to pray, consider these two questions: *Do I need to forgive someone? What do I need forgiveness for?*

If you're open to the Lord, He'll even help you with the answer to those two questions by bringing someone or something to mind. Get things right between you and God so that you can have a great time with Him.

Prayer

Here again we have a topic that books, conferences, and sermons around the world focus on and explore at length. Hundreds of books have been written on prayer. Hundreds of websites are devoted to how you should pray, what prayer should look like, and what you should be praying. It can get a bit overwhelming. Prayer is a vital topic, but we don't have to overcomplicate it. As you walk with God, He will most certainly guide you, and your prayer life will grow and change over the years. What it looks like when you're twenty won't be the same as when you're thirty or eighty.

How long or how often do you pray each day right now? Do you have a specific time set aside? Do you shoot up bullet prayers now and then? If we don't set aside a specific time to pray regularly, we are more likely to simply "pray on the run." Going back to the friend analogy, how close of a friend would someone be if we just swung by, waved hello, and ran off—even if we did it every day? What kinds of things should we share with God? Short answer: everything! Some people even like to keep a prayer journal so they can keep better track of those who need prayer as well as other things the Scriptures remind us to pray for, such as those in authority and our nation. But let's look at a few specific examples just to get us rolling.

- **You can pray about your own life.** Share with God the things that are worrying you or that you care about. Ask Him for guidance about your life and the choices you have in front of you. Remember that piece of paper where you wrote down all your concerns about college? Go ahead and take that out right now and talk to God about what's on that list. Hopefully, you've gotten some information to help you with at least some of those concerns, but we're confident God can help you find the resources you'll need if you stick close to Him.

- **You can pray for those who surround you.** Who in your life needs prayer? The people who surround you are in your life for a purpose, and praying for the needs and concerns of others is a critical part of prayer. You can pray for friends, people who don't know the Lord, your professors, and your campus in general. You can pray for friends back home or at other schools, and you can pray for your family. Your list in this area may change daily as you consider the needs around you.

- **You can pray for the world.** What issues and concerns in the world today has God given you a deep concern about? Abortion? Human trafficking? Adoption? A particular country? Poverty? Politics? The possibilities are endless and we could never individually cover them all, so pray for the ones God has given you a passion for. Along with global concerns, we can also be praying for our nation, our leaders, and our president.

But we don't want to create some list to read off to God. Let Him guide you in prayer so that you can hear what He is concerned about, and talk to Him about those things. For example, maybe when you are praying for your campus, you think of that guy who sits in the front of your English class. Even if you don't know him, it might be God prompting you to pray for him. You may have just read an article on something and God reminds you of it so that you can pray for that issue. Ask God to help you know how to pray and what is on His heart, and He will help guide you through.

Stillness

In the same way we have the opportunity to interact with God in prayer, we have the opportunity to really hear from Him as we spend time with Him. But in order to hear, we have to be really listening, and that takes quiet—not just quiet around us but quiet inside us. We are all so hyper-connected nowadays that we really don't know how to be quiet and still before God. But it's important to learn how to do it. In Matthew, we find that Jesus had this to say about prayer:

Here's what I want you to do: Find a quiet, secluded place so you won't be tempted to role-play before God. Just be there as simply and honestly as you can manage. The focus will shift from you to God, and you will begin to sense his grace. (6:6)

Quiet. Simple. Honest. Aren't those great descriptions?

So how can we practice stillness? Find a way to disconnect. Turn off your phone. Go somewhere quiet where you won't be distracted or disturbed. And don't talk; just listen. Start with only five minutes of complete quiet. If you find your mind drifting, refocus on God and be open to hearing Him. Don't expect some earth-shaking revelation every single day, but if you are willing to be still, you will hear from Him.

Remember, there's no magic formula; it's simply about you and God spending enough time together so that you can get to know Him. He can guide you and change you to become more like Jesus each day.

Spiritual Growth

No one can help you grow spiritually unless you're willing to put in the time to do what you need to do on your end. There's no download button for the Bible, and there's no shortcut to maturity. We simply have to keep walking the steps in front of us with God in the lead. Prayer is just one of the many ways we help keep God in the lead rather than running off in our own direction. Getting into a strong Christian group, becoming a student of the Word of God, and serving others are also valuable tools for helping us grow as Christians.

But doing all of those things doesn't mean that life will be perfect. Don't assume that the road ahead of you will be completely smooth with no bumps. Bumps and valleys are a part of life, and if we're willing to continue to seek God, those valleys can be a beautiful place where we learn to depend on God more fully.

College can be a great time of spiritual growth, and God has given you everything you need to grow into the person you are meant to be. Be encouraged that God is with you and that this grand new adventure you're setting off for can be just that: an adventure with Him!

> May the Lord bless you, guide you, keep you, and sustain you through this next phase of your life. May He lead you into wisdom and guide you in every step you take. May you grow closer and closer to the Lord each day and hear His voice as you study His Word and spend time with Him. May you be a comforting friend, a devoted learner, a wise leader, and a powerful witness of how God works in the lives of His children. In Jesus' name, amen!

Free sample of *The Message//
REMIX Solo* from NavPress

RESOURCES

Dorm Checklist

- Have a safe place to keep valuables.
- Take an inventory of everything you've brought with you to school.
- Create a consistent place to leave messages for one another.
- Check with the school about acceptable and unacceptable items.
- Exchange class schedules with your roommate.
- Post your school's safety procedures.

Packing List

- Eye mask
- Earplugs
- Alarm clock
- Cleaning kit (see page 79)
- Medical kit (see page 82)

Additional Tips from the Trenches

About Packing

- Bring a reading lamp so you can read if your roommate goes to sleep earlier than you.
- Get to know your dorm. How much space will you have? It's really a bummer when you bring all this stuff and suddenly realize you have less space to store it than you thought.
- Be sure to check with your school about items you're allowed to have in your room. Some appliances (even some desk lamps) may be deemed unacceptable and could be confiscated during room inspections.
- Bring plenty of extra things to help you stay organized, such as roll-away drawers, a jewelry organizer, a shoe rack, and plastic bins that fit under your bed. You won't have as much time to clean your room as you think. Anything to help keep you in a routine of organization would be helpful.
- Bring headphones so you can listen to music or watch a movie on your computer if your roommate needs quiet to study.
- Buy a power strip (that acts as a surge protector) to plug multiple electronics into. There are usually only a few outlets in the room, but you'll have many things (refrigerator, computer, printer) to plug in.

About Money

- Spend money wisely! It's really easy to go to the nearest Walmart and get excited that you have some cash and no one to stop you from buying what you want. In college, cash is limited and it goes fast. Keep in mind that you might have to buy gas as well as toiletries and food (depending on the type of dorm you're living in). If you have a meal plan, use it as much as you can. Maybe set aside a small fund for fun stuff such as shopping or bowling and add to it little by little. Don't go too crazy with this newfound freedom.

- Carpool as much as possible. Gas prices are high and college cash flow is low. If you need to make a run to the store, ask if any of your friends need to go. You can take turns with your cars. It saves a lot of money in the long run.

Course Schedule Possibilities Grid

The following chart is a sample of the type of system to use as you plan your courses for the next few years. Create a similar chart on your computer or a separate piece of paper, and list all of the classes you will need to fulfill your course requirements for graduation.

Semester	Possible Class	General Education	Major	Credit
Fall Freshman				
Spring Freshman				
Fall Sophomore				
Spring Sophomore				
Fall Junior				
Spring Junior				
Fall Senior				
Spring Senior				

Bible Reading Plans

A lot of free plans for reading through your Bible are available. While many start on January 1, don't let that stop you from jumping in anytime of the year!

- *Discipleship Journal*, by NavPress, has several downloadable reading plans and a unique plan that requires only five minutes a day: www.navpress.com/dj/content.aspx?id=138.
- Back to the Bible has several reading plans to get you reading and interacting with the Word: www.backtothebible.org.
- Bible Gateway has multiple plans, and you can also get your reading plan delivered to you by RSS, e-mail, or iCal: www.biblegateway.com.

- YouVersion has a free app and reading plans that can be used on your iPad or phone: www.youversion.com.

YouVersion

Books

The Grad's Guide to Surviving Stressful Times, **NavPress, 2011**
A resource for high school grads, this book prepares new college students for the barrage of unfamiliar, stress-inducing situations they may face the minute they set foot on campus. *The Grad's Guide to Surviving Stressful Times* gives sound scriptural advice on topics such as financial responsibility, time management, roommates, and moving to a more independent lifestyle.

The Grad's Guide to Choosing Well, **NavPress, 2010**
The Grad's Guide to Choosing Well helps students wade through the fascinating and frustrating complexities of life and offers guidance in making wise choices.

Everything You Need to Know Before College, **by Matthew Paul Turner, NavPress, 2006**
This survival guide to college explores dating smart, finding friendships, adapting to different personalities, and making the most of your money.

Freshman, **by Mark Matlock, NavPress, 2005**
Are you going to let God be the focal point of your life when you are at college? Will you follow Him even when it's not the popular thing to do? Mark Matlock helps incoming freshmen combine faith and college by encouraging them to think about their faith in new ways.

5 Paths to the Love of Your Life, **by Alex Chediak, Jerusha Clark, Rick Holland, Jonathan Lindvall, Doug Wilson, and Lauren Winner, NavPress, 2005**
Discover five different approaches to dating to discern which one might work for you.

Devotionals

The Grad's Guide to Time with God: Daily Devos for a Deeper Relationship, **NavPress, 2009**
Written for students by students, these creative daily devotions bring the Bible to life in just seven minutes a day. In ten weeks, recent grads will learn new ways of putting their faith into practice.

The Pray! Prayer Journal: Daily Steps Toward Praying God's Heart, **by Dean Ridings, NavPress, 2003**
This prayer-focused journal includes Scripture, a daily Bible reading plan, space to write the names of those you want to pray for, and monthly sections to record insights. With twelve Scripture-based prayer guides, forty-eight devotional readings, and twelve prayers for your spiritual growth, *The Pray! Prayer Journal* is a unique way to grow your communication with God.

Bible Studies

The Faith: A Journey with God, **DFD 2.0**
Designed for group use and written for young adults, this Bible study examines various aspects of the Christian faith, such as God's character, the Rapture, and spiritual warfare. Contains five sessions.

Scripture Memorization

Topical Memory System and *Verseminder*
Use the *Topical Memory System* (TMS), developed by The Navigators, to improve your knowledge of the Bible, deepen your walk with God, and memorize verses that will carry you through the hard times of life. The kit includes

Verseminder

sixty verse cards in the NIV, NASB, MSG, ESV, NRSV, NLT, NKJV, and KJV; a course workbook; and a verse-card holder. Learn more about God and His character as you memorize His Word.

Resource for Self-Injury

Inside a Cutter's Mind: Understanding and Helping Those Who Self-Injure, **by Jerusha Clark with Dr. Earl Henslin, NavPress, 2007**

Cutting is a practice that has crossed age and gender lines. It's not just depressed teens who inflict injury on themselves—it can be anyone dealing with overwhelming feelings. This book explores the complex issue of cutting without offering any pat or simple fixes. It examines the psychology of self-injury, the feelings of anger and despair behind it, and the counseling resources that can help.

For More Information on Sexually Transmitted Infections

- Centers for Disease Control and Prevention, "HIV/AIDS among Youth": www.cdc.gov/hiv/resources/factsheets/youth.htm
- Office of Women's Health: www.girlshealth.gov/body/sexuality/sti.cfm
- WebMD's "The 6 Most Common STDs in Men," by Peter Jaret: http://men.webmd.com/guide/6-most-common-std-men

Hotline Numbers

Suicide: 1-800-SUICIDE

Rape/Sexual Assault: 1-800-656-HOPE

Poison Control: 1-800-222-1222

Campus Police: _____

County/City Police: _____

Doctor's Offices/Hospitals Near My Campus

Office #1: _____

Address: _____

Phone #: _____

Office #2: _____

Address: _____

Phone #: _____

Office #3: _____

Address: _____

Phone #: _____

My Insurance Information

My provider/phone #: _____

My policy number: _____

My co-pay: _____

My coverage: _____

Other important information: _____

My Emergency Contacts

Contact #1: _____

Relationship: _____

Phone number: _____

Contact #2: _____

Relationship: _____

Phone number: _____

Contact #3: _____

Relationship: _____

Phone number: _____

ACKNOWLEDGMENTS

Many thanks to these college students for their Tips from the Trenches!

Shai Caviness, junior at North Central Michigan College

Analicia Davis, senior at Biola University

Arielle Jones, sophomore at University of North Alabama

Ashley L., sophomore at Virginia Tech

Sean McDonough, junior at Oral Roberts University

NOTES

Introduction

1. *Merriam-Webster Online,* s.v. "sacred," accessed August 15, 2011, http://www.merriam-webster.com/dictionary/sacred.

Chapter 1: The Magic Card

1. Lucy Beale and Sandy G. Couvillon, *The Complete Idiot's Guide to Healthy Weight Loss*, 2nd ed. (New York: Penguin, 2005), 102.

Chapter 2: Party All the Time?

1. "A Snapshot of Annual High Risk College Drinking Consequences," *NIAAA*, accessed July 1, 2010, http://www.collegedrinkingprevention.gov/statssummaries/snapshot.aspx.

2. Mayo Clinic Staff, "Symptoms of Alcohol Poisoning," Mayo Clinic, accessed December 10, 2010, http://www.mayoclinic.com/health/alcohol-poisoning/DS00861/DSECTION=symptoms.

Chapter 3: Get Moving!

1. Mayo Clinic Staff, "Exercise: 7 Benefits of Regular Physical Activity," Mayo Clinic, 2009, http://www.mayoclinic.com/health/exercise/HQM01676.

Chapter 5: Risky Business

1. "Facts on American Teens' Sources of Information about Sex," Guttmacher Institute, February 2011, http://www.guttmacher.org/pubs/FB-Teen-Sex-Ed.html.

2. Symptoms compiled from the Office of Women's Health (http://www.girlshealth.gov/body/sexuality/sti.cfm) and the Centers for Disease

Control and Prevention (http://www.cdc.gov/hiv/resources/factsheets/youth.htm).

3. Peter Jaret, "The 6 Most Common STDs in Men," WebMD, accessed December 16, 2009, http://men.webmd.com/guide/6-most-common-std-men.

4. "HIV/AIDS among Youth," Centers for Disease Control and Prevention, accessed August 3, 2008, http://www.cdc.gov/hiv/resources/factsheets/youth.htm.

5. "FAQs: Basic HIV/AIDS Information," AIDS.gov, http://aids.gov/hiv-aids-basics/hiv-aids-101/overview/faqs/.

Chapter 6: Staying Safe On Campus

1. "Male Sexual Assault," RAINN, http://www.rainn.org/get-information/types-of-sexual-assault/male-sexual-assault.

2. "Statistics," RAINN, http://www.rainn.org/statistics.

Chapter 8: Healthy Relationships

1. Jeff Sumpolec, "The ILUV Way," used with permission.

Chapter 9: Struggling with Change

1. "Treatment for Non-Suicidal Self-Injury," NIMH, accessed July 2009, http://www.clinicaltrials.gov/show/NCT01018433.

Chapter 10: A Healthy Mind

1. Donald L. McCabe, Kenneth D. Butterfield, and Linda Klebe Trevino, "Summary: Academic Integrity: How Widespread Is Cheating and Plagiarism?" Restorative Justice Online, 2004, http://www.restorativejustice.org/articlesdb/articles/5778.

2. Cheating statistics compiled by Caveon, http://www.caveon.com/resources/cheating_statistics.htm.

3. *The Bahá'í Faith*, 2011, http://www.bahai.org.

4. Brian White, "A Basic Buddhism Guide: 5 Minute Introduction," Buddhanet, 1993, http://www.buddhanet.net/e-learning/5minbud.htm.

5. *Hinduism Today*, Himalayan Academy, 2011, http://www.hinduismtoday.com.

6. "Introduction to Islam," Islam.com, Inc., 2000, http://www.islam.com.

7. Islam.com, Inc., http://www.islam.com.

8. Sikhs.org, 2011, http://www.sikhs.org.

9. Toa.org, *The Center of Traditional Taoist Studies*, 2009, http://www.tao.org.

10. Unitarian Universalist Association of Congregations, 2011, http://www.uua.org.

11. Promotional Video Content by American Atheists, 2011, http://www.atheists.org.

12. John Smart, "Atheism and Agnosticism," Stanford Encyclopedia of Philosophy, 2004, http://plato.stanford.edu/entries/atheism-agnosticism.

13. World Union of Deists, "Deism Defined," accessed August 15, 2011, http://www.deism.com/deism_defined.htm.

14. "Largest Religious Groups in the United States of America," Adherants.com, 2005, http://www.adherents.com.

The Grad's Guide to . . .

The Grad's Guide to Time with God
TH1NK

Written for students by students, these creative daily devotions bring the Bible to life in just seven minutes a day. In ten weeks, recent high school grads will learn new ways of putting their faith into practice.

978-1-60006-436-4

The Grad's Guide to Choosing Well
TH1NK

As a student, you're faced with making more choices than ever. This resource explores tough issues you'll likely face as you head out for life on your own — sex, future, money, and more — while offering truth, hope, and inspiration to prepare you to make good choices.

978-1-60006-921-5

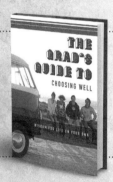

The Grad's Guide to Surviving Stressful Times
TH1NK

Even the brightest graduates may be ill-prepared for the pressures and stress of college life. Keep *The Grad's Guide to Surviving Stressful Times* close at hand and you'll never be surprised by the stressful situations you encounter. Instead, you'll be able to cope with confidence, strengthened by the empowering Scripture verses included.

978-1-61521-607-9

To order copies, call NavPress at **1-800-366-7788** or log on to **www.NavPress.com**.

NAVPRESS

Discipleship Inside Out™